THE FUTURE OF [

A radical manifesto

Gustavo Esteva, Salvatore Babones,
and Philipp Babcicky

First published in Great Britain in 2013 by

Policy Press
University of Bristol
6th Floor
Howard House
Queen's Avenue
Clifton
Bristol BS8 1SD
UK
t: +44 (0)117 331 4054
f: +44 (0)117 331 4093
pp-info@bristol.ac.uk
www.policypress.co.uk

North America office:
Policy Press
c/o The University of Chicago Press
1427 East 60th Street
Chicago, IL 60637, USA
t: +1 773 702 7700
f: +1 773 702 9756
sales@press.uchicago.edu
www.press.uchicago.edu

© Policy Press 2013

British Library Cataloguing in Publication Data
A catalogue record for this book is available from the British Library.

Library of Congress Cataloging-in-Publication Data
A catalog record for this book has been requested.

ISBN 978 1 44730 108 0 paperback
ISBN 978 1 44730 109 7 hardcover

The right of Gustavo Esteva, Salvatore Babones and Philipp Babcicky to be identified
as authors of this work has been asserted by them in accordance with the Copyright,
Designs and Patents Act 1988.

Cover design by Andrew Corbett
Front cover: Painting, based on traditional huipiles woven by
Oaxaca women.
Printed and bound in Great Britain by Hobbs, Southampton

Contents

About the authors

Gustavo Esteva is a grassroots activist and prolific author. He works in collaboration with Universidad de la Tierra, Mexico, and many organizations and networks around the world.

Salvatore Babones teaches sociology and social policy at the University of Sydney, Australia. He has published widely on globalization, inequality, and quantitative methodology.

Philipp Babcicky is a PhD student at the University of Vienna, Austria. His research focuses on environmental sustainability and the sociology of consumption.

Preface

There is universal consensus that we are at the end of an historical era. An old world order is dying and a new world order is being born. But the minute you begin discussing the corpse—just what it is that is dying—you enter into muddy and controversial territory, with all kinds of candidates: full employment, cheap oil (or any oil for that matter), neoliberalism, socialism, capitalism, representative democracy, modernity, postmodernity, even Planet Earth and human civilization, whose end some people announce with a kind of apocalyptic rapture.

In this book we explore the development enterprise and its future (if any), taking into consideration today's peculiar kind of millenarianism. We live in a time of increasing uncertainty. To anticipate the future, which seems so blurred now, many people are turning their faces to the past, in order to find some hope in previous experiences, in crises similar to the current economic crisis. Or they just pray.

"The last forty years can be called the age of development," wrote Wolfgang Sachs in the introduction to *The development dictionary*. "This epoch is coming to an end. The time is ripe to write its obituary." Sachs' book became a paradoxical classic in development studies: people were studying postdevelopment to study development. Twenty years later Sachs wrote in the preface of the new edition of the book: "While discussing the end of the development era in October 1989, we the authors of this book were unaware that at that very moment 'development' had been given a new lease of life."

Was it too soon to write the obituary of development in 1989? In the preface to the new edition, in 2010, Sachs himself argued that, "the age of globalization has now superseded the age of development." And also: "China's success brings the dilemma of the twenty-first century into focus: politics is compelled to push either equity without ecology, or ecology without equity. It is hard to see how this dilemma can be resolved unless the belief in 'development' is dismantled." And he went further. At the end of his preface, Sachs called Gandhi as a witness. In 1926 Gandhi wrote in one of his columns for *Young India:*

> God forbid India should ever take to industrialization after the manner of the West. The economic imperialism of a single tiny island kingdom (England) is today keeping the world in chains. If an entire nation of 300 million took to similar economic exploitation, it would strip the world bare like locusts.

Now, observed Sachs, it is no longer 300 million but 2,000 million in India and across the world setting out to imitate Britain.

One might counter: have we not seen spectacular development and developments in the last 20 years? Do we not face today the historic opportunity to finally eradicate hunger and misery from the planet and to begin a new era of prosperity for everyone? Will not 'sustainable development' finally take care of the environmental problems associated with 'development'? Is today not the day on which the failed promises of development can be finally realized?

Or alternatively, is it the case that development really did die, but there was no funeral and no burial ... and from the rotting corpse all kinds of pests are currently crawling?

We are three very different authors—a Mexican intellectual and activist, an American quantitative sociologist, and an Austrian sociologist studying alternatives to mainstream consumption—who belong to three different generations. We have different viewpoints, begin from different assumptions, and live very different lives. We have never even met together as a group. Nonetheless, we share the same answers to these questions.

For years we have been reading all sorts of literature documenting the natural, social, and cultural disasters associated with development. The facts we use to illustrate our arguments are well known and well documented, but we saw no need to further declaim the damage wrought in the name of 'development'. We did not want to add another horror story to that expansive collection.

Against this background, what we attempt to do in this book may seem impossible or even preposterous. We present a very radical critique of the development enterprise, but without vilifying development scholars or development practitioners. It is not our goal to sow despair. It is our goal to challenge and inspire. We want to offer development scholars and development practitioners a new, more humane, more emotionally satisfying intellectual basis for their vocation.

This is neither a book on development nor a book on postdevelopment. It is perhaps a book on post-postdevelopment, but that would be a silly label. Simply put, this is a book on the world as it is, and as we think it should be. While much of the development literature idealizes US and European modes of development, we do not. Much of the postdevelopment literature eschews the use of statistics as inherently imperialist; we do not. We are not fundamentally interested in ideals and critiques. We are interested in using empirical reality as actually experienced by people around the world today as the basis for reasoning towards realistic suggestions for a better tomorrow.

The word 'development' has a long and convoluted history, and we do not explore this story in our book; there are excellent books and essays covering the field in depth. We do, however, dedicate our first chapter to describing how all the previous connotations of the word were assimilated and transmogrified with the invention of the concept of 'underdevelopment', which transformed the perception of their own condition of the majority of people on Earth. This is not merely a matter of history. The invention of 'underdevelopment' in 1945 underlies many damaging preconceptions about development that continue to limit our ability to imagine what we want for our futures, or even what is possible for the future.

Today the word 'development' itself lacks any specific meaning. It has no specific denotation. The technical uses of the word float like debris on its ordinary language meaning and make it incomprehensible. Development used to allude to a logical

—

sequence of thought, such as the awakening of a child's mind or the opening of a flower. It has become the equivalent of a grunt, a cipher, an algorithm, deriving its meaning from the words associated with it, from the tone used when it is pronounced and from the context in which it is applied.

The word, however, is full of connotations. For the majority of the people in the world it usually implies escaping from a vague, indefinable, and undignified condition, and it is still the emblem for an enterprise that destroys both physical environments, and human cultures all over the world. We describe in our first chapter the usually ambiguous and ambivalent reactions to such enterprise, how it evolved, and the main trends in the attitudes about development.

Chapter Two is dedicated to a reflection on development statistics. We examine some of their uses and misuses by way of illustrating how they are designed and produced according to the interests and ideologies of the institutions supporting their production. The real wellbeing of living people is often disregarded. We also refocus the available statistics to demonstrate how they can offer a picture of the world that is radically different from the conventional perceptions they are generally used to support.

In Chapter Three we explore the recent evolution of the development enterprise and the emergence of alternatives through which millions of people have begun to affirm and implement their own paths for social transformation and fulfilment.

In Chapter Four we rigorously examine the realities and perceptions associated with demography and the environment as they relate to development. We explore the meaning and implications of the Malthusian concern with population increase (and control), and how they may be turned upside down when confronted with real data on people's uses and abuses of the Earth's environment. Scarcity and sustainability are examined in depth.

In Chapter Five we describe the ongoing insurrection (for such it is) in a time in which the development enterprise has taken the shape of what David Harvey has called 'accumulation by dispossession.' Real social change does not happen as a series of cataclysmic moments associated with great leaders but through daily transformation conceived and implemented by ordinary people. We dedicate this chapter to exploring how, in different spheres of reality (eating, learning, healing, settling, and exchanging), people are taking innovative initiatives and enriching their existing traditions in new adventures of transformation, sometimes for sheer survival, other times in the name of old ideals, and most of the time challenging the dominant paradigms and structures.

Chapter Six describes how an old word, 'commons', gets a new meaning in the epic movements now unfolding at the grassroots level around the world. The enclosure of the commons in Britain is conventionally considered the beginning of capitalism. It has accompanied the spread of capitalism around the world and is manifest today in specific areas of confrontation—for example, around land seizure for strip mining and plantation agriculture. Some people were able to resist enclosure and keep their commons; they are now working to regenerate them. Some other people lost their commons but have recently succeeded in reclaiming them. And still other people, who do not have anything they can call a commons or even a community, are recreating their social realities and giving the word a new meaning in the creation of new commons.

At the end of this radical manifesto against the development enterprise as it has historically played out, in Chapter Seven we share our own vision of how development scholars and development practitioners can contribute to making the world a better place. Scholars and practitioners don't have to become cynics or abandon their profession or field of study. They can live rewarding lives and play positive roles in social transformation, both in their own places and in the other places they are passionate about. But to do so they must challenge the preconceptions they have inevitably internalized simply by living in the world in which we live. We ourselves—the authors of this book—continually challenge each other to fight off these pervasive preconceptions.

We ask development scholars, development practitioners, and people everywhere to think more broadly about what is desirable and what is possible for the future of the multiple worlds that must coexist on this single planet.

We hope that the readers of this book will enjoy the adventure of reading it as much as the authors have enjoyed the adventure of writing it. We have written from places as far from each other as Mexico, Australia, and Austria. We have constructed a virtual community and a real friendship in our adventure of writing. We hope that you will construct equally rewarding communities and friendships in your adventures of reading, discussing, and (yes) disagreeing with what we have written.

Publisher's note: The authors have directed that all royalties earned from sales of this book be contributed to the Universidad de la Tierra, Oaxaca, Mexico.

ONE

The birth of development and underdevelopment

Development is at the center of a powerful but fragile semantic constellation. It shaped the dominant mentality of the second half of the 20th century, which can thus be legitimately called the era of development. Today the word has lost any specific, universally accepted meaning, but it is still loaded with connotations. This very emptiness helps to explain why it is still fashionable in public discourse. At the top, governments, international institutions, and corporations are still involved in what they label as the development enterprise. At the grassroots, many people are still struggling for incorporation into the 'developed' world—with many different ideas and fantasies about what it is. An increasing number of people, however, are not only resisting both specific developments and development itself but they are also following again their own paths and creating new worlds, new shapes of society. The time has come to listen to them and learn with them what it is to be beyond development, why you can choose such an option without going backwards or falling into fundamentalism, and how you can join them.

In fact, by development many people say the opposite of what they mean to convey. On the one hand, 'development' is a word used for something good: we study development because we want everyone to share in it; we want more of it; we see the 'underdevelopment' of **less-developed countries** (LDCs) as a curse to be lifted through the application of modern scientific knowledge, economics, and industrial production. 'Development' means that everyone has access to clean drinking water from a convenient home tap; every child has the opportunity to attend 12 or more years of school; mothers can give birth in a clean environment attended by qualified medical personnel; no one need suffer from malnutrition or other preventable diseases; everyone uses a flush toilet. Policies of rich countries that hinder or prevent the development of LDCs are selfish, bordering on criminal.

On the other hand, 'development' is a word used for something bad: we fight development because we want to save people from it; we want less of it; we see the 'underdevelopment' of so-called LDCs as a prelapsarian state of grace to be preserved against the encroachments of modern so-called civilization. 'Development' means that natural water resources are polluted by industrial and human waste; schools are used as a tool to obliterate indigenous languages and cultures and autonomous learning; mothers are cruelly separated from their children at an early age; previously healthy populations are afflicted by an onslaught of diabetes, hardening of the arteries, and tobacco-related disease; everyone has to start buying toilet paper, tampons, and a range of disposable consumer products. Rich country policies that promote or encourage the development of LDCs are selfish, bordering on criminal.

At the end of the Second World War the US was the richest country in the world, according to economic historian Angus Maddison's *Contours of the world economy 1-2030 AD* (Oxford University Press, 2007), by far the richest country that had ever been in existence on Earth. It was undisputedly the center of the human universe. The **International Monetary Fund** (IMF) and the institution that was to become **The World Bank** were headquartered in its capital city, Washington DC. The **United Nations** (UN) met in its commercial capital, New York, and modelled its Charter on the preamble to the US Constitution. The US Navy was absolute master and commander of the Earth's oceans. The US was the universal creditor, an amazing productive machine producing half of the world's measured economic production, and enjoyed a way of life that, as Hollywood was explaining to everyone, was very close to paradise. The US was the only major power that was physically undamaged by the war. It had the Bomb.

But the US—and Americans—wanted something more. They wanted to make entirely explicit their new position in the world. And they wanted to consolidate that hegemony and make it permanent. For these purposes, they conceived a political campaign on a global scale to remake the world in America's image, or at least in America's image of America's image. In 1949 America's newly elected President, re-elected after a fashion but only for the first time elected in his own right, was understandably intent on establishing his identity, his 'brand' as we might say today, his legacy.

The man who dropped the Bomb had never been elected to do so. **Harry S. Truman**, 33rd President of the US, inherited the Second World War and America's awful burden when his overwhelmingly charismatic boss **Franklin Delano Roosevelt** died on 12 April 1945. Just four months later he became the first and only person in history ever to order the use of atomic weapons in war. The ensuing three-and-a-half years of his accidental presidency were unavoidably focused on dealing with the aftermath of a decade of world war.

In January 1949 Truman and the US were ready to open a new era, a uniquely American era. On 20 January, he delivered his presidential inaugural address. In it he laid out a four-point agenda for the postwar world. The first point was to support and expand the UN. The second point was to continue the rebuilding of Europe. The third point was to establish the organization now known as NATO (**North Atlantic Treaty Organization**). These first three points together constituted the solidification of America's postwar military alliances against the Soviet Union. Truman's fourth point dealt with the rest of the world:

> Fourth, we must embark on a bold new program for making the benefits of our scientific advances and

industrial progress available for the improvement and growth of underdeveloped areas.

More than half the people of the world are living in conditions approaching misery. Their food is inadequate. They are victims of disease. Their economic life is primitive and stagnant. Their poverty is a handicap and a threat both to them and to more prosperous areas.

For the first time in history, humanity possesses the knowledge and the skill to relieve the suffering of these people.

The United States is pre-eminent among nations in the development of industrial and scientific techniques. The material resources which we can afford to use for the assistance of other peoples are limited. But our imponderable resources in technical knowledge are constantly growing and are inexhaustible.

I believe that we should make available to peace-loving peoples the benefits of our store of technical knowledge in order to help them realize their aspirations for a better life. And, in cooperation with other nations, we should foster capital investment in areas needing development.

Our aim should be to help the free peoples of the world, through their own efforts, to produce more food, more clothing, more materials for housing, and more mechanical power to lighten their burdens.

We invite other countries to pool their technological resources in this undertaking. Their contributions will be warmly welcomed. This should be a cooperative enterprise in which all nations work together through the United Nations and its specialized agencies wherever practicable. It must be a worldwide effort for the achievement of peace, plenty, and freedom.

With the cooperation of business, private capital, agriculture, and labor in this country, this program can greatly increase the industrial activity in other nations and can raise substantially their standards of living.

Such new economic developments must be devised and controlled to benefit the peoples of the areas in which they are established. Guarantees to the investor must be balanced by guarantees in the interest of the people whose resources and whose labor go into these developments.

The old imperialism—exploitation for foreign profit—has no place in our plans. What we envisage is a program of development based on the concepts of democratic fair-dealing.

Exactly two weeks later the Communists took Beijing. In August the Soviet Union tested its first atomic bomb. On 7 December 1949—a day that may ultimately prove more significant than 7 December 1941—Chiang Kai-shek effectively conceded mainland China to the Communists by proclaiming Taipei his provisional capital. By 1950 a new era was already underway.

The creation of underdevelopment

America's commitment to "development based on the concepts of democratic fair-dealing" was stillborn into the Cold War. From the beginning the top two recipients of US **official development assistance** (ODA) foreign aid were Turkey and Greece, their stability necessary to prop up the southern flank of the newly formed NATO alliance. Later the biggest ODA targets would be Egypt and Israel, buying a peaceful supply of Middle Eastern oil. Today the big three US aid recipients are Afghanistan, Pakistan, and Iraq. So much for development based on democratic fair-dealing.

By using the word 'underdeveloped' to describe most of the world's landmass and peoples, Truman changed the meaning of development and created the symbol, a euphemism used since then to allude discretely to the overwhelming fact of US hegemony. In 1949 the vast majority of the people of the third world did not live "in conditions approaching misery"—certainly not by the standards of 1940s. In 1949 malaria was still endemic in the southern US. Sugar, meat, and gasoline were rationed in

—

the UK. Germany and Japan were in ruins. Development was created as a symbol of affluence, a promise of what life could be like under a benign US imperium. Development meant anti-Communism.

Development as a symbol turned out to be gifted with an unbeatable malleability. Nowadays no one accepts the Truman conception of development. Neither the Americans nor the anti-Americans presently use the word to express a meaning equivalent to what Truman expressed. But none of the political and intellectual contortions to which the word has been subjected during the last six decades has succeeded in dissociating the word 'development' from the connotations that it acquired on 20 January 1949. Those who have been more explicit about opposing Truman's plans (starting with **Joseph Stalin**) and those who have intensely tried to distance themselves from the kind of domination evoked by 'development' have only succeeded in rooting the symbol more deeply. It appears to possess the virtue of transforming all opposition, all failure, and all neglect into opportunities for buttressing itself.

The time has come to reveal its secret.

Development has a long and convoluted history; underdevelopment, a very short one. Most observers (scholars, politicians, professionals, pundits) observe underdevelopment everywhere. They rarely ask themselves why. Even those who remember the ideological origins of development and underdevelopment fail to apply that memory to inform their observations. Faith, as the poet Antonio Machado used to say, is not to see something or to believe in something, but to believe that one sees.

Most observers, of course, believe that they themselves are observing what they observe. They rarely try to identify the social subject casting, through them, a subjective glance on very diverse realities, in order to qualify them through disqualification, comparing and judging them before seeing them. They think they are using their 'own' eyes and never notice the collective glasses placed on them without their permission.

Underdevelopment began on 20 January 1949. On that same day, two billion people became underdeveloped. In a sense, from that time on, they ceased being what they were, in all their diversity, and were transmogrified into an inverted mirror of others' reality: a mirror that belittles them and sends them off to the end of the queue, a mirror that defines their identity, that of a heterogeneous and diverse majority, in the terms of a homogenising and strict minority.

Truman was not the first to use the word. Wilfred Benson, a former member of the Secretariat of the International Labour Organization, was probably the one who invented it when he referred to the 'underdeveloped areas' while writing on the economic basis for peace in 1942. But the expression found no further echo, neither with the public nor with the experts. Two years later the Austrian economist Paul Rosenstein-Rodan wrote of 'the international development of economically backward areas' (his enumeration of which, interestingly, did not include South America). Throughout the 1940s the expression appeared occasionally, here and there, in technical books and official documents. But it only acquired relevance when Truman presented it as the emblem of his own policy. In this context, it took on an unsuspected colonizing virulence.

In 1949 the postwar world order was taking shape. On one side was the 'first world' made up of the US and its new NATO alliance. On the other side was the 'second world' of the Soviet Union and the victorious Mao's China. The majority of the world—the **third world**—was rapidly decolonizing, and it was anyone's guess what direction it would take. Already in 1949 it was obvious that the British and French colonial empires were crumbling. India, the richest and consequently the most exploited colony in the world, had gained independence in 1947 and promptly descended into civil war. The Netherlands never fully reasserted control over Indonesia after the Japanese withdrawal. The pre-war colonial world order was over. Truman's famous Point Four was his attempt to stamp on the world the terms on which the postwar American world order would be born.

Since Truman, development connotes at least one thing to revolutionary and missionary alike: to escape from the undignified condition called underdevelopment. When Mexican human rights activist Rodolfo Stavenhagen proposed ethnodevelopment, or development with self-confidence, conscious as he was that we need to "look within" and "search for one's own culture" instead of using borrowed and foreign views, when Nigerian environmentalist Jimoh Omo-Fadaka suggested a development from the bottom up, conscious as he was that all strategies based on a top-down design have failed to reach their explicitly-stated objectives, when Colombian sociologist Orlando Fals Borda and Bangladeshi economist Anisur Raman insisted on participatory development, conscious as they were of the exclusions made in the name of development, when they and so many others qualify development and use the word with caveats and restrictions as if walking in a minefield, they do not seem to see the counterproductivity of their efforts. The mines have already exploded.

In order for someone to conceive the possibility of escaping from a particular condition, it is necessary first to feel that one has fallen into that condition. For those who make up two thirds of the world's population today, to think of development requires first the perception of themselves as underdeveloped, with the whole burden of connotations that this carries. They are not living outside the planet, as if nothing had happened since 1949. Today, for two thirds of the peoples of the world, underdevelopment is a threat that has been carried out, a life experience of subordination and of being led astray, of discrimination and subjugation.

Through the new metaphors of alternative developmentalists, in fact, the colonizing virulence of underdevelopment is spread and rooted even more deeply. It penetrates areas of popular mentality where Truman's designs never could have reached or even imagined, thus complementing his work. They literally underdevelop those who had succeeded in resisting the previous models or concepts of development, and those who, after falling into the colonized kind of conscience created by these models and concepts, had been persistently trying to escape from it. For two thirds of the people on earth, this positive meaning of the word development—profoundly rooted after two centuries of social construction—is a reminder of what they are not. It is a reminder of an undesirable, undignified condition. To escape from it, they need to be enslaved to others' experiences and dreams.

Ivan Illich on America

Ivan Illich was a historian, philosopher, priest, theologian, and social critic born in 1926 in Vienna, Austria.

In the 1970s Illich became known as a radical critic of modern institutions, all of which had become, for him, counterproductive: they produce the opposite of what they are supposed to produce. He applied the motto "the corruption of the best is the worst" to many of them, starting with the Catholic Church. His critical observations of the real outcome of the systems of education, health, and transportation produced immediate scandal, but only anticipated what today is common sense and conventional wisdom. In *Tools for conviviality* (1973) he extended his critique to the industrial mode of production and its political institutions, and gave new meaning to the word 'conviviality' to describe how a postindustrial society would be constructed by coalitions of the discontented in the time of the crisis, when all those counterproductive institutions would begin to collapse, thus anticipating what seems to be happening today.

Illich identified 'radical monopolies' colonizing or inhibiting people's autonomous abilities to learn, heal, walk, or shape their homes and environments, thus creating dependency on products and services provided by private or public institutions. He urged common folk to reclaim their autonomy and self-determination, as well as their sense of proportion, in order to discover through friendship that dependence on things or tools could destroy, rather than enhance, graceful playfulness in personal relations. In a similar vein, Illich criticized North America's ideological colonization usually disguised as services, brought by 'do-gooders.' He deemed the 'US idealist' the third largest North American export next to money and guns. He was one of the first to formulate an open critique of the development enterprise.

Illich described the idealistic tendencies of Americans in a famous essay, 'Violence: A mirror for Americans.' Originally published in 1967, it was included in his 1969 book *Celebration of awareness*. In it he wrote:

> The compulsion to do good is an innate American trait. Only North Americans seem to believe that they always should, may, and actually can choose somebody with whom to share their blessings. Ultimately this attitude leads to bombing people into the acceptance of gifts. In early 1968 I tried with insistence to make some of my friends understand this image of the American overseas. I was speaking mainly to resisters engaged in organizing the march on the Pentagon. I wanted to share with them a profound fear: the fear that the end of the war in Vietnam would permit hawks and doves to unite in a destructive war on poverty in the Third World.

What might Illich say today about America's 'reconstruction' of Iraq and Afghanistan?

Conceptual conflation: development and growth

The concept of development was further tarnished in the hands of its early promoters, who conflated development with specifically economic development and ultimately with measured rates of economic growth. In the 30 years leading up to Truman's inauguration, the US economist Simon Kuznets (and others) had been working on setting up a **System of National Accounts** (SNA) for the US economy. These accounts focused on the calculation of **gross domestic product** (GDP) and its close cousin, **gross national product** (GNP), both of them measures of the total economic output of a country.

Kuznets was well aware that national economic output was not a measure of national wellbeing. But what kind of output? At what cost to the people, to communities, to the environment?

The father of national income accounting himself testified before the US Senate in 1934 that "no income measurement undertakes to estimate the reverse side of income, that is, the intensity and unpleasantness of effort going into the earning of income. The welfare of a nation can, therefore, scarcely be inferred from a measurement of national income as defined [in GDP statistics]." Nonetheless, the first major statistical effort of the new UN was to standardize the US SNA and to roll it out across the globe. Soon GDP statistics were being produced for all UN members, with European and US technical assistance provided for new member states. Measures for GDP, GDP per capita and annual GDP growth rates came to be available for most countries by the late 1950s, and immediately became the key metrics by which 'development' was judged.

British orientalist Bernard Lewis' 1955 dictum that 'first it should be noted that our subject matter is growth, and not distribution' reflects the mainstream emphasis on economic growth which permeated the whole field of development thinking. Paul Baran, by far the most influential development economist among the leftists, wrote in 1957 on the political economy of growth, and defined growth or development as the increase in the per capita production of material goods. W.W. Rostow, who had a very impressive impact on the institutional thinking and the public, presented his 'non-Communist manifesto' in 1960 as a description of the stages of economic growth, assuming that this single variable may characterize the whole of society—and, incidentally, keep Communism at bay. All of these authors, of course, dealt with much more than just economic growth, but their emphasis on growth in national income per capita reflected the spirit of the times ... and the crux of the matter.

By the end of the 1960s, however, many factors contributed to dampen the optimism about economic growth. The shortcomings of current policies and processes were more conspicuous than at the beginning of the decade; the list of putative prerequisites for growth was relentlessly expanding; and it became clear that rapid growth was much more difficult

—

11

in practice than in theory. By then, the economists were more inclined to acknowledge 'social aspects' or, more often, 'social obstacles.' Conceptually, there was a generalized revolt against the straitjacket of economic definitions of development that constrained its goals strictly to quantitative indicators of material output.

The question was clearly posed in 1970 by former US Defense Secretary Robert S. McNamara, then recently departed to head The World Bank. After recognizing that a high rate of growth did not bring satisfactory progress in development during the 1960s, he insisted that development policy in the 1970s broaden its focus. But this 'dethronement of GNP,' as the crusade was then called, did not go very far: no international or academic consensus was possible on any other definition. The conceptual straightjacket of measurement is more powerful than any critique. The more people struggle against it, the tighter the straps become. There have been too many critiques of GDP for any of them individually to be taken too seriously. National income statistics are deeply embedded in the global data infrastructure; they continue to be measured every year, and, as the aphorism says, what gets measured gets done.

All of which didn't look so bad for the emerging professional development establishment centered on UN institutions and The World Bank. From the beginning of GDP measurement, and from the beginning of independence for the post-colonial countries that now started measuring their GDP, growth in GDP per capita as recorded in World Bank statistics was very rapid pretty much everywhere around the world. In the 1960s and 1970s, the less-developed countries (LDCs) of the world were developing—at least by the measure of growth in GDP per capita.

Then came Paul Volker, the tight-money **Federal Reserve** and the increase in US interest rates to a record-high prime rate of 21.5 per cent in 1981. Since the whole world outside Europe and Japan borrowed in dollars, the Federal Reserve monetary tightening of 1979-82 represented a massive economic shock that was beyond the control of national governments. The result was two recessions in the US and one long depression in the rest of

—

the dollar-denominated world. The neoliberal revolution, with the dismantling of all the social arrangements associated with the New Deal, had begun.

The 1980s were called 'the lost decade for development' in Latin America, but the same was true for Africa, the Middle East and most of the rest of the world. In those years the word 'development' covered a wide collection of contradictory practices conceived as quick answers for every crisis, but in fact it was a frayed flag. By the 1980s no country dared to propose that the United Nations should sponsor a new Development Decade. Even the original impetus to Truman's development program—fighting the Communist threat—disappeared with the decision of the Chinese Communist Party to embark on the 'capitalist road' in 1978, the collapse of the socialist states of Eastern Europe and the dissolution of the Soviet Union in 1991, and the opening of India's economy beginning in 1991. In 1992 Wolfgang Sachs wrote the 'obituary' of development in his introduction to *The development dictionary*. **Postdevelopment**, whatever that meant, seemed an idea whose time had come.

And yet ... GDP per capita continued to be measured every year, year after year, for every country. Theorists might proclaim the death of development and empirical reality might show that development through GDP growth had failed not only in its ultimate goal of improving people's lives through GDP growth but also in its immediate goal of GDP growth, but the World Bank, the UN, and the global panoply of development non-governmental organizations (NGOs) didn't magically go out of business. And GDP per capita continued to be measured every year, year after year, for every country. No one measured 'postdevelopment.'

So the 1990s saw the rise of the **Washington Consensus**. It was not an explicit agreement. It was the convergence of Washington-based institutions, particularly the IMF, the World Bank, and the US Treasury, to express the hegemony of the only remaining superpower in terms that eliminated all previous discretion about its connection with corporate power. John Williamson, an economist at the private Peterson Institute who

---

coined the expression in his 1990 book *Latin American adjustment: How much has happened?*, expressed the idea in very clear terms:

> The economic policies that Washington urges on the rest of the world may be summarized as prudent macroeconomic policies, outward orientation, and free-market capitalism. It practices the last of these with more consistency than the first two, but that should not be taken to imply that they are less important. Most of technocratic Washington believes that the failure to practice what is preached hurts the United States as well as the rest of the world.

The Consensus was not a set of policy objectives but a collection of policy instruments, such as smaller government, the elimination of trade barriers, privatization, deregulation, fiscal discipline, and the state enforcement of property rights (especially for foreign investors). Development is not mentioned as a goal or even as a consequence, but it is assumed that it will be a natural outcome of such orientation. Once 'getting the policies right' becomes the priority, however, it is possible to radically delink the development enterprise from people's actual wellbeing, a political operation already prepared by the identification of development with GDP growth and nothing else.

By 2000 it was clear to everyone outside Washington that Washington Consensus policies did little for GDP growth and mostly worked to further the exploitation of the poor by the rich. If GDP per capita stubbornly refused to grow, the development establishment would set new goals that would. Economist Jeffrey Sachs, the villain of the early 1990s Washington Consensus sell-off of Soviet industries from an oligarchic government into the hands of private sector oligarchs, sought redemption by championing the new **Millennium Development Goals** (MDGs). Who could oppose reductions in hunger, the elimination of childhood diseases or increases in women's empowerment?

With the promulgation of the MDGs in 2000, the half-century arc of development rhetoric came full circle back to Truman. In 1949 President Truman proclaimed that:

—

More than half the people of the world are living in conditions approaching misery. Their food is inadequate. They are victims of disease. Their economic life is primitive and stagnant. Their poverty is a handicap and a threat both to them and to more prosperous areas.

On 18 September 2000 the UN General Assembly resolved that:

We will spare no effort to free our fellow men, women and children from the abject and dehumanizing conditions of extreme poverty, to which more than a billion of them are currently subjected. We are committed to making the right to development a reality for everyone and to freeing the entire human race from want.

The eight MDGs were designed to resolve themselves. First, although they were promulgated in 2000, progress towards them was backdated to 1990: success in meeting the MDGs would be measured based on improvements from 1990 to 2015. The timing was no accident. Starting in 1990 meant a running start, since many of the selected indicators had improved in the 1990s. Rapid GDP growth in China and India (together representing some 40 per cent of the world's population and over half of the world's poor population) was also underway by the early 1990s. Whether due to the efforts of the UN or simply the background advance of technology, the world will be able to report massive progress towards meeting the MDGs between 1990 and 2015.

To the extent that 'development' meant making the world more American through the adoption of the American way of life as a universal ideal, it has succeeded. But it has entirely failed, even in Truman's terms, if we consider the real outcomes of this operation, particularly in terms of people's wellbeing.

"For the first time in history," he said, "humanity possesses the knowledge and the skill to relieve the suffering of these people," the majority of people on Earth. Indeed. Technical and material means are currently available to prevent hunger and other basic deprivations everywhere. But far from relieving the suffering

—

15

of the lesser developed, modernizing their poverty has, in many ways, deepened it.

"The old imperialism—exploitation for foreign profit—has no place in our plans," Truman declared. "What we envisage is a program of development based on the concepts of democratic fair-dealing." Observing how many times development programs have been associated with the police, the support of dictatorships, and the repeated violation of the sovereign will of the weak, no one can seriously argue today that the development enterprise has been "based on the concepts of democratic fair-dealing."

And finally, if the implicit purpose of development was to extend and to give stability and legitimacy to the American hegemony, it has also failed: one of the main challenges for every US president today is to explain to the people why the US no longer has the position and role it had in the world and how they will deal with the consequences.

At the end, more than 60 years after the beginning of the era of development, it looks like an experiment that in the experience of the world majority has miserably failed.

The fantasy that everyone in the world secretly (or avowedly) wants to be an American is still a strong conviction for many Americans. It is difficult for them to imagine that what the US wants for the world might not be what the world wants for itself. This was, no doubt, Truman's conviction. He already understood in 1949 that development meant the use of the world's resources and labor by rich investors based mainly in the US and other first world countries. He did, after all, conclude his four-point program by emphasizing that:

> Such new economic developments must be devised and controlled to benefit the peoples of the areas in which they are established. Guarantees to the investor must be balanced by guarantees in the interest of the people whose resources and whose labor go into these developments.

He didn't question whether or not it was right that the US should plunder the world for its resources and labor. He merely offered to be fair in doing so. Even on that modest criterion it is hard to argue that development has lived up to its promise.

The invention of scarcity and the creation of needs

The MDGs grew out of the **basic needs** approach to development. This approach itself never became an accepted international strategy because no consensus could be reached about a universal definition of basic needs, but needs-based orientations brought a touch of realism to the development enterprise. While the goals of development were unfeasible and the universalization of the US way of life remained as a distant ideal, it seemed possible to at least satisfy the basic needs of people everywhere. After some estimates of the resources needed for that purpose were prepared, this more modest goal seemed indeed feasible, and soon became ingrained in thinking about development aid. Once upon a time development aid might have been targeted toward infrastructure projects or the support of scientific research, but today it goes largely unquestioned that its purpose is to help meet the basic needs of the less-fortunate who are unable to meet those needs for themselves ... among other reasons, because of development aid.

For the modern mind, needs are part and parcel of the human condition. But in the modern meaning they are very modern indeed: they emerged with the arrival of capitalism, with the enclosure of the commons in 18th-century England and everywhere else soon thereafter. In reality, however, basic needs—as defined today—are a modern fiction.

The readers of these words do not need air: you are all breathing. But if you were suddenly thrown into the ocean, you would soon be in desperate need of air. A catastrophic destitution, dispossessing people of their way of life, is the precondition for every modern 'need' (and thus the root cause of modernized poverty). Market society operates through the creation of scarcity, which in turn shapes all needs, usually through dispossession.

In their enjoyment of the commons, individual people had few immediate 'needs' as these are understood today. When

—

everyone has the right to share in the bounty of nature, no one has individual needs that are not at the same time shared needs. The community may enjoy more or less abundance, but the community eats or starves together. In the commons, a natural disaster might create a sudden shortage of water, food, clothing, or shelter, which may lead to suffering and death. But since England's **Great Charter of the Forest** in 1225, English commoners got the guarantee that their means of subsistence would be respected, and they would thus be able to satisfy by themselves their own necessities. In a literal sense they had no needs, except when a natural disaster caused a shortage they could not handle or overcome. When the commons were enclosed—in effect, privatized—the commoners were deprived of their guaranteed means of subsistence. They were thus thrown into the labor market to find money for water, food, clothing, and shelter. Natural disasters were no longer the main source of need—lack of money became the main source. And this is the origin of modern needs.

Economist Amartya Sen became famous for showing in his 1981 book *Poverty and famines: An essay on entitlement and deprivation* that the countries that experienced some of the worst famines of the 20th century were exporting food while their people were dying of hunger. Strip mines, palm oil plantations, and even large-scale shopping centers are all modern forms of the enclosure of the commons. From its beginning in 18th-century England, the enclosure of commons has never stopped.

Contemporary economists have educated the world into the view that the economy is as old as the hills, an unavoidable condition of all human society. The founding fathers of economics saw scarcity as the cornerstone of their discipline. They postulated it as a universal condition of human society, with axiomatic value. This economic way of thinking is now so immersed in common sense that it is very difficult to perceive that the premise of scarcity is socially manufactured, not naturally pre-existing.

Economists predicated the law of scarcity on the technical assumption that people's desires are infinite, whereas their means are limited (although improvable). This creates the economic problem *par excellence*: the allocation of resources (means) to competing, unlimited desires (ends). Open markets and planned economies are contrasted as alternative ways to allocate resources. Academic dispute on their respective efficiency will go on for ever, but in the real world, in both capitalist and socialist countries, it always involves a combination of the two.

In many societies and cultures, even today, the idea of wanting more than what you have is perceived as something immoral or foolish. People's desires, in any case, are socially determined, and the assumption that they recognize no limits is an assumption, not an axiom. What the people want and the amount of what they want depends on cultural contexts and circumstances. In the 1950s most Americans had no practical limits placed on their food consumption, but consumed much less food than Americans of the 2000s, and were much healthier for it. Individual desires only become infinite when the option of infinite desire is framed and promoted to individuals through advertising and ideology.

A billion people will go to bed tonight with an empty stomach. Millions are dying of curable diseases. Homelessness is proliferating. There is a complex set of factors causing this tragic condition of the world, prominent among them the ecological consequences of the development enterprise. In many ways all these forms of scarcity are manufactured. For many years now the world has had the material and technical means to overcome any local shortage caused by natural disasters. There is no need for any community to be in need.

People who are seriously interested in alleviating other people's suffering should begin by asking themselves if they are directly or indirectly contributing to that suffering.

Basic needs and *buen vivir*

If one expression could capture the main meaning of social movements currently flooding Latin America it would be *sumak kawsay* (Quechua), *suma qamaña* (Aymara), *boa vida* (Portuguese) or *buen vivir* (Spanish). *Buen vivir* is 'the state of living well.' The definition and construction of what it is to live well was traditionally in the hands of society, in the people themselves. Such responsibility was transferred to government in the modern nation-state, which in time turned it over to the corporations. Traditional society in Latin America and throughout the third world has held it to be the responsibility of the people construed at the face-to-face level, in every urban *barrio* or every rural community.

Over the past 60 years development ideology has substituted a universalized identification of what it is to live well with living conditions as experienced by the middle classes of the first world. It soon became evident that the adoption of such a way of life by the peoples of the third world was unfeasible, on socioeconomic and environmental grounds. The goal of development was thus pragmatically shifted to ensuring the satisfaction of basic needs rather than graduation to a US-style middle-class **standard of living**. The US has proved itself politically incapable of bringing all of its own citizens to this level of affluence; that it should show the political will and the economic and practical capacity to bring the majority of the world to such a condition is unthinkable.

It is impossible and illegitimate to compare different notions of living well and to declare one of them better or worse than the others. US middle-class norms are increasingly exposed to criticism, particularly for environmental and health reasons, but many people still adhere to them. The idea of transcending development is not a form of reverse imperialism, trying to impose on them an alternative view. But today millions, perhaps billions of people are resisting development in all its forms, and affirming themselves on their own paths, culturally and locally defined. It is no longer acceptable (if it ever was) to continue to impose on them an outside definition of what it means to live well.

In substituting nouns for verbs—learning for education, healing for health, eating for food—people are reclaiming their own agency in communal settings. Sometimes these are their own original commons they were able to preserve or reclaim and sometimes these are new commons created in an urban context by those who lost their original communities in the 20th-century rush towards urbanization. For them, *buen vivir* is an idea based on a verb: it is life lived well, a principle realized in action. It puts the emphasis on doing, rather than consuming.

- *Eating.* Some people are afraid of hunger and some others of eating—they don't know what is in the food they are buying and ingesting. Cultivating food in the cities (urbiculture) and new arrangements between farmers and urban consumers defines a vigorous trend that is clearly associated with the idea of food sovereignty as defined by the peasant movement **Via Campesina**. Despite all the challenges it faces, Cuba is today the world champion of organic agriculture, and half of the food eaten in its cities is produced in them.
- *Learning.* The educational system is not delivering—it does not prepare people for life or work and marginalizes the majority. Many people still struggle to 'get education,' in many meanings of the expression. Many others go beyond the institutional framework, recover ancient traditions of apprenticeships, and introduce contemporary technologies in learning and studying as free leisure activities.
- *Healing.* Health systems around the world are inefficient, discriminatory, and increasingly counterproductive. New notions of health and new perceptions of body and mind are nourishing autonomous healing practices, recovering traditions marginalized and disqualified by the medical profession and enabling healthier behavior and more humane treatments that are well rooted in families and communities. Healthy living is far more effective at preventing most diseases than the most powerful drugs are at curing them.
- *Settling.* Social and ecological disasters associated with large-scale housing developments (including the informal slums created by marketization) are common, and often lead to the proliferation of homeless people. Today there is a countermovement aimed at recovering and consolidating traditional settling practices that once defined urban growth in Latin America. Contemporary technologies, particularly those inspired in environmental concerns, are now enriching those initiatives.
- *Knowing.* New centers for the autonomous production of knowledge, usually independent of official government research centers and universities, are emerging everywhere. They generate new technologies and theoretical innovations, reformulating perceptions of the world and introducing methodologies challenging dominant paradigms. Indigenous and practical knowledge, until recently disqualified, marginalized, and threatened with extermination by modernizers, is now treasured and applied in innovative ways.

—

Development as practice

German postdevelopment theorist Wolfgang Sachs — somewhat ironically writing in the journal *Development*—called development 'a concept of monumental emptiness.' Such statements are commonplace in academia—they are not fringe views. Surely students, policymakers, and the public have a right to be confused! Why are the so-called development experts so hostile to development?

Given the fractious state of the field, it is worth reminding ourselves and our readers that development scholars are, by and large, well-intentioned. These good intentions are often what drew them to the field. The same cannot be said of chemists or medievalists, who may be good people but are not generally people who were inspired by their goodness to pursue their chosen studies. It is a rare development scholar who simply finds the problem of development academically 'interesting.' From Wolfgang Sachs on the left to Jeffrey Sachs on the right, development scholars want to make our world a better place.

Most thinking on development today can be categorized into one of three approaches, which might be called 'the three Sachses of development.'

The first approach, which expresses a pretty general consensus in economics, politics, and society outside academia, is the *Goldman Sachs approach*. While academics struggle to define 'development' in theory, Goldman Sachs and its peers in the banking, mining, engineering, and oil industries, define development in practice through their commodities trading desks, their infrastructure projects, and their exploration units. These companies staff government offices on a rotating basis, endow the think tanks that promote their interests and employ more lobbyists to work on development-related issues than there are academics working in development studies departments. These companies are 'strategic partners' (that is, major funders) of the **World Economic Forum**. The press interviews them and their hired representatives whenever their interests are at stake. The Goldman Sachs approach is absolutely hegemonic outside academia at the top of the society. In this approach, development means an oil platform located at least 10km offshore, safe from harassment by local indigenous militants.

A (relatively) ragtag band of academics, activists, and celebrities espouses a second approach, called here the *Jeffrey Sachs approach* after its most prominent proponent. It is also the approach of Bob Geldof, Bill Gates, and many other well-meaning people around the world, and includes the major US and European development NGOs. The Jeffrey Sachses also include the more progressive wing of the economics establishment, those found staffing development institutes rather than business schools. Its adherents focus mainly on the alleviation of obvious suffering—they stand for a chicken in every pot, a mosquito net over every bed, and a condom on every penis. The Jeffrey Sachs approach may not be hegemonic in New York, Washington, or Davos, but it is well respected. When the press needs an interviewee to represent the 'good guys' on development, they go to the Jeffrey Sachses—often to Jeffrey Sachs himself. They love to discuss this kind of philanthropic capitalism.

The Goldman Sachs strategy for accomplishing its development aims is based on the principle of *divide et impera*, while the Jeffrey Sachs strategy of poverty alleviation seeks to put minimal humanitarian limits on the *et impera* portion of that formula. These two approaches, pushed forward mainly by corporations and NGOs, reach an uneasy equilibrium in which successful development means maximum economic exploitation accompanied by a minimum of premature deaths among the people being developed. The end result is a world of zombies ruled by vampires.

The third approach, the one closest to the vision presented in this book, is the *Wolfgang Sachs approach*. It is now deeply entrenched in academic development studies departments (confusingly, postdevelopment is usually what is taught in these departments). In addition to academics, members of this group include indigenous leaders, documentary filmmakers, and independent intellectuals. The adherents of this approach are relatively little-known outside their own circles, rarely cited in

—

the media and almost never found in positions of direct influence over policy. They are rarely found as featured speakers at the meetings of intergovernmental organizations and are never invited to the Davos World Economic Forum. They are often caricatured as being against poverty alleviation. Dambisa Moyo, who has worked for The World Bank and for Goldman Sachs, is not one of the Wolfgang Sachses.

Much of the sometimes-vicious controversy plaguing development studies today has to do with the tension between the Jeffrey Sachses championing the need to make sure that individual people are able to stay alive and the Wolfgang Sachses championing the need to make sure that people can live in living societies. This tension is not endogenous to development studies but provoked by the actions of the Goldman Sachses, which are the root causes of pressing humanitarian needs to be met. The Jeffrey Sachses aren't the ones manufacturing scarcity; they're just trying to meet the resulting needs. Sadly, the Goldman Sachses' strategy of *divide et impera* has been as effective against development scholars as it has been against the people being developed.

Many social movements, involving millions and perhaps billions of people, have already adopted this third approach. This is not to say that they are aware that an academic literature exists to support their endeavours. As Wolfgang Sachs makes clear in his writing, they aren't following Wolfgang Sachs; Wolfgang Sachs is following them. For sheer survival or in the name of old ideals, at the center of megacities or in isolated villages, in the most diverse settings, ordinary people, usually without leaders or parties, are courageously taking their lives once more into their own hands.

The time has come to listen to these people. Many, perhaps most, development scholars, students, even practitioners, are in the field because they want to contribute to make the world a better place and they feel real compassion for the less fortunate, for those in pain, for those who are suffering. The time has come to join them in their courageous struggle to affirm themselves on their own path instead of trying to help them to follow an alien, even counterproductive, path.

Recommended reading

Arndt, H.W. (1978) *The rise and fall of economic growth: A study in contemporary thought*, Chicago, IL: University of Chicago Press.

Arndt, H.W. (1987) *Economic development: The history of an idea*, Chicago, IL: Chicago University Press.

Frank, A.G. (1966) *The underdevelopment of development*, New York: Monthly Review Press.

Max-Neef, M., Elizalde, A. and Hopenhayn, M. (1992) 'Development and human needs,' in P. Ekins and M. Max-Neef (eds) *Real-life economics: Understanding wealth creation*, London: Routledge, pp 197-213.

Rahnema, M. and Robert, J. (2008) *La puissance des pauvres* [*The power of the poor*], Paris: Actes Sud.

Rist, G. (2001) 'L'invention du développement,' *L'ecologiste*, vol 2, no 4, pp 19-22.

Rist, G. (2002) *The history of development: From western origins to global faith*, London: Zed Books.

Rostow, W.W. (1960) *The stages of economic growth: A non-Communist manifesto*, Cambridge: Cambridge University Press.

Sachs, J. (2005) *The end of poverty: Economic possibilities for our time*, New York: Penguin Press.

Scott, J.C. (1998) *Seeing like a state: How certain schemes to improve the human condition have failed*, New Haven, CT and London: Yale University Press.

Sen, A.K. (1999) *Development as freedom*, Oxford: Oxford University Press.

Shorrocks, A and van der Hoeven, R. (eds) (2004) *Growth, inequality, and poverty: Prospects for pro-poor economic development*, Oxford: Oxford University Press.

Stavenhagen, R. (1996) *Ethnic conflicts and the nation state*, New York: St Martin's Press.

—

TWO

Development statistics and what they tell us

According to official World Bank statistics reported in its **World Development Indicators** (WDI) database and report, one third of the world's population lives on less than US$2 a day. Forty per cent of the world's population don't have a flush toilet and 60 per cent don't have indoor plumbing. Countries accounting for less than 15 per cent of the world's population garner over 60 per cent of the world's total income. Life expectancy at birth, which runs to over 80 years in much of Europe, is still under 50 years in much of Africa. Activist NGOs report that factory conditions in China are in some cases the functional equivalent of slave labor—or worse. If we believe Transparency International's corruption index, the 100 most corrupt countries in the world are all outside Europe and North America. According to the IMF's annual *World Economic Outlook*, the US is 10 times as rich as Bolivia, and Bolivia is 10 times as rich as Zimbabwe. The widely cited Polity IV Project considers only about 60 per cent of the world's countries to be democratic, and the NGO Freedom House considers fewer than half the world's countries to be 'free.'

At first glance, the world's development statistics seem to paint a depressing picture. But first impressions can be deceiving. A bedrock principle of the international data infrastructure is that organizations collect data in support of their missions, not for the edification of the world. Thus, economic data are collected in extraordinary detail because intergovernmental organizations such as the IMF and The World Bank need economic statistics to feed their business models—and they are willing to pay to make sure they are collected. Demographic and health data have smaller but still powerful constituencies. Cultural data are much less important to governments and intergovernmental organizations, and environmental data can be downright embarrassing.

The pictures we have of the state of the world are inevitably based on the data that are visible, and since those data represent the interests of the powerful, the pictures are inevitably the pictures of the powerful. It is difficult to tell the stories of the majority when the majority don't report statistics. Want to know the taxes collected on goods and services as a percentage of value-added in Malaysia in 2010? No problem: 3.90 per cent (WDI 2012 dataset). Want to know the median household income anywhere in the world? Sorry, not collected. Want to know what proportion of pharmacy medicines is authentic? Sorry, not collected. Want to know how many people participate in the arts? Sorry, not collected. As a result, lack of development ends up meaning a lack of the things the data collectors think you should be purchasing, since that is all we have statistics for.

The view of the world that emerges from development statistics also depends on how the pictures are framed. Seen from the relative comfort of an upper-middle-class home in Surrey or Massachusetts, even Wales or Rhode Island might seem an unpleasant place. On the other hand, seen from the cultural vibrancy of Rio or Accra, suburban US and Britain might seem a grotesquely bloated wasteland populated by fat, lonely people who derive little meaning from their tightly controlled lives. This is not meant to deny the existence of poverty in the world. Clearly, there is real poverty in some parts of the world. But just as clearly there is serious overconsumption in other parts of the world. The rhetoric of development problematizes the former while glorifying the latter. A more even-handed balanced framing of the development picture might reveal some interesting insights.

Instead, the entire development literature (so far as we know without exception) frames the issue of development from the

—

standpoint of those who haven't needing to catch up with those who have. The US and Europe are ahead; the rest of the world is behind. The task of development theory and practice is to guide 'the rest' toward catch-up with the West. This is how Truman framed the issue, and over the ensuing six decades no one has thought to take the picture out of the frame. Both the developers and those they classified as 'underdeveloped' internalized this perspective on the human condition. The challenge of development is the challenge for the poor to catch up to the rich. New York and London represent the normal, healthy state of humankind. By comparison, Accra and Rio are diseased.

A shift in perspective

A shift in perspective shows the same picture in a whole new light. What is the 'normal' state of human living on Earth in the early 21st century? Surely it isn't life as lived in the US and Europe. In many ways life in the US and Europe is very nice, but statistically it is just as extreme as life in India and most of Africa. Neither the penthouses of Manhattan nor the villages of Uganda represent ordinary ways of living on our planet. So how does the ordinary human live?

To begin with, the ordinary, according to WDI data, median human being lives in a country that has about US$5,000 in national income per person. China, the Dominican Republic, and Algeria are all roughly ordinary places to live. Mexico's national income per person is twice the world average, Sri Lanka's about half. National income per person in the US is about nine times the level experienced by the world's median person. Europeans are similarly pathological.

In many ways it must be very nice for Americans and Europeans to command such high income levels, but the implication of this is that they place enormous burdens on the planet. One indicator of this is the level of carbon dioxide emissions per person. Again, according to the WDI, the median person in the world lives in a country with three tonnes of emissions per person

—

per year. That's roughly the level of emissions in the Maldives, Cuba, or Egypt. Carbon dioxide emissions in France are about twice this level, in the US about six times. No one knows exactly how much carbon dioxide can be safely reabsorbed by the environment, but it's a sure bet that three tonnes is more absorbable than 18 tonnes.

Again, relying on WDI data, the world's median life expectancy is 72 years, about the level of Brazil, Egypt, and Latvia. Only about 20 per cent of the people in the world live in countries with life expectancies of greater than 75. The median is thus very close to the maximum life expectancy. All the money in the world doesn't buy (much) more life. Two thirds of the people of the world live in countries where life expectancy is over 65 years. Nearly all of the people of the world with lower life expectancy live in South Asia and sub-Saharan Africa.

Further data from the WDI report that more than half the people of the world live in countries where the infant mortality rate is less than 20 per 1,000. That's 0.2 per cent. About two thirds of the people of the world live in countries where the infant mortality rate is less than 50 per 1,000 (0.5 per cent). Again, South Asia and sub-Saharan Africa are the exception.

On the other hand, WDI data suggest that at the global median national income of around US$5,000 per person year, more than 90 per cent of the population is literate, more than 90 per cent of children receive required immunizations, and more than 90 per cent of the urban population has access to potable water.

Put all the angles together, and the picture starts to resolve itself. The typical person living in the world today lives in a country where the national income per person is around US$5,000. In that country, people are able to live long, healthy lives without putting too much stress on the world and its ecosystems. These are the world's ordinary people, the people this book is mainly about. If the whole world lived like they live, the world would be a pretty decent place.

On either side of them, about 20 per cent of the world's people live in grotesquely opulent or grotesquely deprived conditions. The word 'grotesque' is used here advisedly. The 20 per cent who live in houses with three bathrooms, three television sets, and three-car garages are destroying the world; not coincidentally, they are destroying the worlds of the 20 per cent who live with no bathrooms, no television sets, and no bicycles, to say nothing of SUVs. These two grotesques are organically linked: the one creates the other. Mexico produces the richest man on Earth, and some of the poorest. These are not two phenomena, but one phenomenon with different consequences for different people.

In most of the global South, in the US$5,000 a year countries, life for most people is full, healthy, and productive. Real poverty arises mainly where Northern consumption demands collide with Southern subsistence lifestyles. Where these worlds collide—where there are coalmines, palm oil plantations, oil drilling, sweatshop factories, commercial aquaculture—it is subsistence that makes way for consumption.

As with the 18th-century enclosures of the commons, the poverty created in the South doesn't necessarily appear in the actual areas that have been appropriated to subsidize the lifestyles of the North. By definition, people forced off their land must live somewhere else. Thus the problems appear in seemingly untouched rural areas or in the shantytowns on the edges of cities. Either way, the root causes of most of the grotesque forms of poverty in the global South are not ignorance, corruption, or mismanagement in the global South. It is more often the ignorance of Northern consumers, the corruption of Northern corporations, and the mismanagement of Northern regulators.

Nonetheless, poverty remains the exception rather than the rule, the grotesque rather than the norm. True wellbeing goes unmeasured in the international development statistics, but the abnormality of poverty is revealed by the tension between two statistics that we do have. Two of the UN's MDGs are to end poverty and to end hunger. According to the UN's own MDG progress evaluation, between 1990 and 2008 the number of people in the world who lived in extreme poverty (on less than US$1.25 a day) fell from over 2 billion to 1.4 billion. Yet over that same period the number of people who were undernourished rose from 817 million to 850 million. How can malnourishment

—

be rising when the number of people in poverty is declining so rapidly?

The answer is that poverty is measured in terms of money, usually money spent (consumption). If you live on communal land and grow your own food, you may be poor but well fed. If you are forced off your land and go to live somewhere else where you have to earn money to pay rent and buy food, you are no longer poor but you may be poorly fed. It's nearly impossible to exist in the market economy anywhere in the world on less than US$1.25 a day. Thus 'poverty' by construction tends to measure the percentage of people who live outside the market economy rather than the percentage of people who live poorly. By forcing people into the market economy, development lifts them out of 'poverty,' officially defined. But does it improve their lives? Would you rather be poor or hungry?

Palm oil, biodiesel, and starvation

Until recently, biofuel was seen as the environmental panacea, a renewable source of energy helping to cut greenhouse gases and providing a route out of poverty for small-scale farmers. Today, the picture looks much more sober as the detrimental socioeconomic effects of biofuel production have come to the fore. Palm oil farming, for example, is found to cause large-scale deforestation, reduce biodiversity, and destroy the natural basis of subsistence farmers. In numerous cases the introduction of large-scale palm oil plantations leads to the displacement of subsistence farmers, forcing them to migrate into more urbanized areas, only to find themselves caught up in slums, desperately looking for paid income.

The propagated positive effects on global warming have also been largely overestimated—the contribution of biofuel to mitigating climate change has proven to be only marginal. Research published by the US Environmental Protection Agency (EPA) in its January 2012 report in the *Federal Register* has shown that biofuels emit only 11-17 per cent less greenhouse gases than conventional fuels over their lifecycle. This effect is so small that the EPA has suggested that palm oil should no longer be classified as a renewable fuel.

Regardless of the established negative effects of palm oil production, the lucrative biofuel business is booming. According to a July 2012 report in *Nature* magazine, Indonesia is currently "the largest grower of oil palms" and "is expected to double production by 2030." Developing countries around the world are increasingly cutting down forests and transforming arable land into more profitable biofuel crops. Malaysia, the world's second largest grower of oil palms, is running out of land and desperately looking for ways to make more land available for new palm oil plantations. Again, according to *Nature*, large-scale producers based in Malaysia have already begun to reach beyond the country's borders towards Cambodia and Indonesia.

The motives behind booming palm oil production are various. Palm oil is used in processed food, cosmetics, soap and shampoos, and as a key ingredient in paints, pesticides, lubricants, and cleaning products. The increasing demand of biofuels is another major cause for cutting down forests to make way for palm plantations. Although the European Union (EU) has just recently discovered and admitted that biofuel production causes detrimental environmental and social problems, its guidelines still require member states to raise the biofuel share of total road transportation fuels to 10 per cent by 2020.

Perfectly legally and economically justified, the production of biofuel continues to boost food prices, worsening hunger and accelerating global warming. In reality, biofuel production only increases global demand of agricultural land, which otherwise could be used to grow edible food and provide resources for people who desperately need them. Instead, official policies permit countries to cut down rainforests, drain peat land, displace small-scale farmers, and produce millions of tonnes of additional carbon emissions.

Living and dying

The most basic indicators available in the international data infrastructure are data on births and deaths, and thus on **life expectancy**. Life expectancy is not a metaphysical projection

—

based on the likely progress of medical science over the coming decades. It is a straightforward arithmetic calculation based on current death rates for people of any given age at any given time. Life expectancy at birth is thus only tenuously connected to how long a person can expect to live. It is a backwards-looking figure estimated at birth based on past statistics, not a forward-looking figure estimated for adults based on future statistics.

The starting point for life expectancy calculations is the **life table**, which might more aptly be called a death table. Life tables report age-specific death and survival rates in any one year. For example, US Census Bureau figures show that in 2008 in the US 0.681 per cent of all live-born infants died before reaching one year old, giving an infant mortality rate of 6.81 per 1,000 live births. Among one-year-olds, 0.045 per cent died before reaching age two. Among two-year-olds, 0.028 per cent died before reaching age three. The age-specific death rate for the US reaches a minimum of 0.008 per cent for 10-year-olds, then starts to climb again. By age 99, Americans have about a 30 per cent chance of dying before reaching 100.

Freezing statistics in time at 2008 death rates, the life expectancy of an infant born in 2008 is estimated by integrating all the age-specific death rates for 2008 to arrive at a composite life expectancy. Life expectancy thus means something like 'under current conditions, how long would today's newborns likely live?' In 2008, the answer for the US was that a newborn baby could look forward to 78.0 years of future life. But for a one-year-old, the remaining life expectancy was 78.6 years. In other words, by living to one year old, infants in the US increased their overall live expectancy from 78.0 years to 78.6 years.

Because of the very high rates of infant mortality, deaths due to war, due to episodic events (such as famines), and due to AIDS, life expectancy in many sub-Saharan African countries can be extremely volatile. In Liberia, for example, life expectancy in 1995 was just 28 (according to US Census Bureau estimates). By 2010 it had risen to 57, an increase of almost two years of life expectancy every year. That would seem to make people nearly immortal: a 20-year-old in 1995 may have just eight years to live, but that same person in 2010 would be 35 and have a further 22 years to live.

Of course, it doesn't really work that way. Life expectancy at birth fluctuates because the age-specific death rates of older people are fluctuating. In Liberia, the under-five mortality rate decreased from a staggering 35.7 per cent in 1995 to a much lower (although still very high) rate of 11.5 per cent in 2010. By contrast, life (and death) for adults changed much less, with the death rate for Liberians in their forties dropping from around 0.7 to 0.6 per cent per year. In countries that have under-five mortality rates in excess of 10 per cent (100 per 1,000 live births), life expectancy at birth is strongly influenced by infant and child deaths.

All of which is not to say that infant and child deaths are not tragic. But for most of the people actually living in a country at any given point in time, the overall life expectancy at birth isn't really a very relevant statistic for describing how long or how well they will live. For example, according to World Health Organization (WHO) estimates, life expectancy at birth in Cambodia in 1999 was less than 54. But total life expectancy for Cambodian 20-year-olds was 64—and even that doesn't factor in the improvements in nutrition and medical care that the Cambodian person is likely to have experienced in the ensuing years. Those Cambodian 20-year-olds of 1999 are probably likely to live into their late sixties.

By comparison, the same WHO estimates placed French life expectancy at birth at just over 79 and French total life expectancy at age 20 at just under 80 years. The French 20-year-old gained less than one additional year of life expectancy for having made it through childhood (versus 10 extra years for the Cambodian). The 20-year-old Cambodian of 1999 certainly can't expect to live as long as the 20-year-old French person of 1999, but the difference is relatively small considering the enormous gulf in national income separating the two countries: IMF statistics report that France has roughly 50 times the national income per person of Cambodia.

—

Higher levels of national income are associated with longer lives. France has 50 times the income of Cambodia, and a French adult can expect to live perhaps 15 years longer—but that is an extreme example. Comparing France to the global middle, France has about five times the income of Mexico, but a French adult can expect to live just three years longer. That is a very large disparity in consumption to finance a few extra years in an old-age home.

The real failure of the international data infrastructure, however, is that what little we know about life expectancy only covers the quantity of life, not the quality of life. The WHO has made some efforts to produce statistics on **disability adjusted life years** (DALYs), but these statistics tend to medicalize quality of life. They implicitly operationalize 'whole life' as 'life free of disease' without any regard for the kind of lives people live. So, for example, is a life spent quarantined in a resettlement camp of the same quality as a life spent in the forest? It might very well be longer, but does that make it better?

It is easy to download data on life expectancy from an internet source and to use it to represent a country, to make a point, or to extol the success or damn the failure of a policy. The statistic is not meaningless, but it is not very nuanced.

The ultimate indicator: GDP per capita

Life expectancy is an important statistic, and one might think it would be the main focus of writing on development. After all, without life, what else matters? The development ethos, however, is at heart an economic program, not a human one. Almost the entire development literature focuses on just one statistic, the indispensable statistic, the ultimate indicator: *GDP per capita*. The talismanic letters G D P stand for gross domestic product, the sum total of goods and services produced or provided within a country's borders; per capita literally translates from Latin as per head and means per person. The statistic GDP per capita is thus gross domestic product divided by population.

GDP is measured as the sum total monetary value of all of the goods produced and services provided in a country. By definition, the only goods and services that count in GDP are goods and services that are paid for. Thus, GDP (a measure of production) is conceptually equivalent to national income (with some minor technical adjustments) and is generally discussed as such. Other measures, such as gross national product (GNP) and gross national income (GNI), are conceptually similar. All conventional indicators of national income basically measure the same thing: the amount of value created in a country, expressed in monetary terms.

Several perversions of GDP are well known. For example, cigarette sales add to GDP—national income is generated when people buy things, not only when people buy good things. When cigarettes make people sick, their visits to the doctor add to GDP. Long, lingering deaths from diseases such as lung cancer generate much more national income than quick deaths from accidents. Accidents don't generate GDP, but rebuilding after accidents does. If you drive your car for 20 years without incident you fail to contribute to your country's GDP; if you have an accident requiring major repairs, you generate growth in the car repairs sector. For years Japan boosted car sales by virtually requiring (through onerous inspections) that people replace their perfectly good cars every three or five years.

Perhaps the most egregious perversion of GDP is military spending. The US alone spends US$700-$800 billion on military programs (depending how you count). Every bomb dropped and restocked by the US military adds to US GDP; the rebuilding of the houses, property, and people damaged by US bombs adds to the GDP of the receiving country. Wars always generate spending. The bigger the war, the higher the spending.

Then there are the things that are left out of GDP: keeping a house, raising families, growing food (to eat, not to sell), enjoying time off, sleeping. Anything that does not have a dollar value attached to it is not included in GDP. When such non-market spheres are brought into the market, GDP grows. So when a peasant changes from growing her own food and

—

giving the surplus to neighbours to growing commercial crops for sale on the market, GDP rises. When a peasant is displaced by a commercial farm and has to go and live in a nearby city shantytown, working for pay in the informal economy so she can afford to pay for food and housing, GDP increases even more.

Even a low productivity commercial farm plus a low productivity displaced peasant laborer generates infinitely more GDP than a subsistence farmer on her own land. If the newly displaced peasant attracts international aid money, all the better: that generates foreign exchange in addition to GDP. In relatively unmonetized poor countries, social catastrophe is the surest way to generate GDP growth.

Dividing overall GDP by population produces GDP per capita. All people are used in this calculation, including children, older people, people with disabilities, and people of all kinds who do not participate in the market economy. Even though the numerator of GDP per capita is the size of the market economy, the denominator is the entire population. This creates obvious distortions in poor countries where large numbers of people work on the land or otherwise do not fully participate in the market economy. Interestingly, however, it is now starting to distort perceptions of some of the very richest countries' economies.

In Japan the proportion of the population aged 65 and over rose from 12 per cent in 1990 to 23 per cent in 2010. On current trends, it is expected to rise further to 32 per cent in 2030. The international development community consensus is that this represents a demographic time bomb, and in fact growth in Japanese GDP per capita has been relatively slow since 1990.

The ageing of Japan's population has meant a slowing in Japanese GDP per capita growth. Hearing the alarm bells being rung by the development establishment (the IMF, the OECD, etc.) one would think that Japan had been hit by an economic and democratic crisis worse than Fukushima. But decade after decade Japan's GDP keeps growing, even in per capita terms, despite the fact that more and more people are retired. Is it really so bad for Japan that it maintains the highest life expectancy and the highest standards of living in the world while fewer and fewer Japanese people have to work in the market economy? Is it really so bad for Japan that elderly Japanese can retire in peace?

Ironically, one of the 'problems' facing Japan is that its retirees are so healthy that they don't seem to require the high levels of expensive medical and nursing home care that Americans do. So many Japanese retirees live simply and peacefully at home, walking and gardening, that they have become a drag on GDP growth. If the goal of a country is to live well, Japan has succeeded as few others. If the goal of a country is to generate an expansion in GDP per capita, Japan is turning into a complete failure.

National income (GDP) per capita is the ultimate development indicator. It is so widely used as a measure of national wellbeing that it has come to mean 'national wellbeing.' News reports routinely report GDP growth as if it were an end in itself; even academics are usually guilty of the same negligent reasoning. Although GDP per capita is not without its uses, it should always be remembered that GDP is no more and no less than a technical measure of the size of the monetary economy.

Growth in GDP is not necessarily a bad thing. Sometimes the monetary economy can grow through people improving their productivity in good ways. When a farmer learns how to improve productivity through intercropping while at the same time enriching the soil, both GDP and human wellbeing increase at the same time. All too often, however, the indicator becomes the goal: policies are pursued purely to promote GDP growth rather than to promote human wellbeing. This practice is especially endemic in poor countries, since by far the easiest way to increase GDP in a poor country is to monetize something that had previously been non-monetary. The conversion of subsistence agriculture into cash crops, the conversion of free water collection into payment for captured sources, the conversion of free people into paid workers will always, by definition, boost GDP. They are unlikely, however, to improve people's lives.

—

Alternative measures of national wellbeing

Regardless of all the criticism and scepticism, GDP remains the dominant measure of socioeconomic wellbeing (at least in the sphere of national accounting). In recent years, however, numerous efforts have been made to create new and most notably more representative indicators of human wellbeing, with yet limited success. One of the most prominent approaches is the Human Development Index (HDI). Often praised as an alternative measure of wellbeing, the indicator was introduced by the UN Development Programme (UNDP) in 1990 and is published annually in the UNDP's *Human Development Reports*. The HDI is a composite index of health, education, and income indicators aiming to rank countries in terms of their 'human development.' The underlying idea is to shift the focus of policymakers and development practitioners away from purely economic to actual human wellbeing.

This approach has not been without criticism. Some have argued that the underlying statistical methods and data errors would not allow an accurate classification of countries along the common 'low,' 'medium,' 'high,' or 'very high' categories. Formula changes, arbitrary categorization thresholds and cut-off values are not only diminishing a meaningful year-to-year comparability but also intriguing countries to deliberately undertake strategic actions only to move up in future reports. To account for some of the criticism, an inequality-adjusted HDI (IHDI) was introduced in 2011 by factoring in inequality in the distribution of each dimension across the population. Today, despite these efforts, many critics regard the HDI as having the same rich-country bias as GDP.

Other alternative indicators of national wellbeing have been offered by the measures of Gross National Happiness, the Happy Planet Index, the Satisfaction with Life Index, or the Genuine Progress Indicator. Although most of the alternative indicators successfully include broader aspects of human wellbeing, none has ever lived up to the dominating popularity of GDP.

What has been left out of the equation in most of the wellbeing measures are ecological and resource consumption considerations: these indicators do not usually account for the socio-environmental costs human development imposes on the global biosphere or on distant countries. It proves to be much more difficult to create indicators of national wellbeing that measure countries on the degree to which they create the conditions for human flourishing without destroying those conditions for others. For example, rich countries have only 10 years' higher life expectancy than middle-income countries (much of it spent sick or in hospitals) but at the cost of five times the greenhouse gas emissions. Besides the obvious difficulties in measuring non-impact wellbeing, the real problem lies in the lack of incentives for the powerful countries to measure something on which they would score poorly.

Ginis, medians, and purchasing power parities

Measured by GDP per capita as reported by the IMF, Equatorial Guinea is now the richest country in Africa. It is a country of half a million people (although this is disputed) on the west-central coast of Africa, surrounded by Gabon (GDP per capita US$11,000) and Cameroon (GDP per capita US$1,200). After the discovery of oil in the 1990s, Equatorial Guinea's GDP rose dramatically, reaching US$27,500 per capita in 2011 (depending on how many people you believe live in Equatorial Guinea—no one really knows). Equatorial Guinea's GDP per capita is now higher than South Korea's and closing in on New Zealand's. The GDP per capita of the neighbouring country Gabon is similarly bloated by oil, although not to quite the same degree.

But Equatorial Guinea is no South Korea or New Zealand (nor is Gabon a Poland or Argentina). By its own low national standards, some 77 per cent of Equatorial Guinea's population lives in poverty. According to WDI data only about 14 per cent of the adult population has a bank account. Around 36 per cent of all employed people are employed in the army. Fewer than half of children receive standard immunizations, and only a quarter of AIDS sufferers are receiving care. Less than 10 per cent of the population uses the internet. Only 52 per cent of children finish primary school on time.

—

How can a country that is almost as rich as New Zealand have a primary school dropout rate of 50 per cent? In a word: inequality. In Equatorial Guinea (as in many countries that are effectively governed by the major multinational oil companies) a small elite garners nearly all of the country's oil income. Everyone else—everyone except the political rulers, their courtiers, and those who serve them—is worse off. Gaining no benefits from oil wells, they must deal with the consequent land seizures, water pollution, and price distortions. All for one and nothing for all.

Inequality is usually measured using a statistic called the **Gini index**, named for its inventor, the Italian statistician (and fascist apologist) Corrado Gini. The Gini index measures the degree of concentration in a country's income distribution. It represents the percentage of inequality in a country on a scale from 0 per cent (everyone has exactly the same income) to 100 per cent (one person gets all of the country's income). No one knows the Gini index in Equatorial Guinea, but it is probably the highest in the world.

According to official US statistics, the Gini index for US households is 48 per cent. That is to say, the US is almost mid-way between perfect equality and perfect inequality. By international standards, that's actually pretty unequal. According to Eurostat data, the Gini index in France is about 30 per cent, in Sweden, 24 per cent. Brazil, one of the world's most unequal large countries, has a Gini index of 53 per cent, down from a high of 60 per cent in the 1980s.

A high Gini index throws an additional wrench into the interpretation of GDP per capita. According to US official statistics, US GDP per capita is about US$48,400. Not all of that national income goes to individuals (some of it is reinvested), but personal income per capita is around US$41,700. That means that, in principle, enough income is earned in the US for every man, woman, and child to receive US$41,700 every year.

Ranking all households in the US from poorest to richest, the income of the middle or **median** household is US$50,050. The US Census Bureau reports that the median US household has 2.55 living in it. Thus, the income of the median US household is roughly US$19,600 per person (give or take a few thousand dollars for technical issues related to the incommensurability of medians). That's less than half the US GDP per capita of US$48,400 or the US personal income per capita of US$41,700. Because of the high levels of inequality in the US, the living standard of the typical American is far lower than a simple intuitive judgement based on GDP per capita would suggest. The even higher levels of inequality in Equatorial Guinea result in far lower typical living standards than might be suggested by GDP per capita.

All this suggests that GDP per capita is a hazardous indicator of incomes in society, even for highly monetized economies such as that of the US. But at least US incomes are measured in US dollars. When we evaluate other countries, the **developmentalist** practice is to always compare them to the US—in US dollars. The IMF, The World Bank, and OECD, and even the UN, use only one currency to report incomes: the dollar. This raises the important question of how all those other GDPs per capita should be converted into dollars.

The obvious answer is to convert all other currencies into dollars using market **exchange rates**. After all, GDP represents only the monetary economy, and if markets are good for anything they're good for measuring the monetary economy. The IMF and some other organizations do use exchange rates to convert non-US GDP into dollars. But the vast majority of official sources—and, perhaps most importantly of all, Wikipedia—use a different measure. They convert other currencies into dollars based on **purchasing power parity** (PPP).

When non-US GDP is converted into dollars using market exchange rates, the conversion is straightforward: if 1 Singapore dollar buys 0.795 US dollars, Singapore's GDP per capita of S$63,050 becomes a US dollar GDP per capita of $50,125. The problem is that exchange rates change daily (or second-by-second) and can swing wildly from year to year. To address these problems, economists have developed PPP exchange rates based on the principle that the same basket of goods should be worth the same amount in every country. The *Economist* magazine's

—

famous Big Mac Index, which it uses to evaluate whether other currencies are overvalued or undervalued relative to the dollar based on the price of a McDonald's hamburger, is a simple form of PPP adjustment.

It is more than a little ironic that many of the institutions that have done the most to promote market fundamentalist views of the world should not trust market exchange rates and instead put their faith in PPP estimates based on local price surveys done around the world. That said, PPP indexes surely have appropriate uses. Unfortunately, comparing different countries' standards of living using GDP per capita is not one of them.

The problem with using PPP exchange rates to compare GDPs per capita is that they have a built-in bias that flatters high inequality countries. High inequality countries already look better than they are because their GDPs per capita outstrip their median incomes. But PPP exchange rates make the situation even worse. The calculations behind PPP exchange rates are based on the overall consumption patterns in society, not on the consumption patterns of the typical consumer. In a relatively equal country, these are roughly the same thing. In very unequal countries, however, most consumption is consumption by the rich. The consumption of the poor doesn't matter much in determining the PPP exchange rate.

Worse, unequal countries by definition have very low wages, which makes it possible for the rich to consume an inordinate quantity of services (personal maids, personal cooks, gardeners, chauffeurs, etc.). The cheapness with which one can hire a maid makes it look as if the cost of living in that country is very low, when in fact the cost of living may be very high—for maids. Putting all these effects together, PPP exchange rates dramatically flatter the statistics of highly unequal countries with high poverty rates. In other words, they flatter poor countries—and the US.

Of the 177 countries for which PPP exchange rate estimates were available for 2010, GDP per capita increased when PPP rates were used in 155 of them and decreased in only 22. The 22 countries that seemed less wealthy when using PPP rates were 19 rich European countries, Japan, Venezuela, and Suriname.

—

The first 20 were relatively egalitarian rich countries, while the last two were partly socialist middle-income countries. It is no coincidence that PPPs made these countries look less attractive, the US and other impoverishing countries more so.

Taken together, high inequality, the difference between per capita and actual median income, and the distorting effects of PPPs make the GDP per capita statistics reported on the world's websites even less meaningful. Certainly, they are meaningful, but they mean much less than is commonly assumed. Policies that improve living standards may improve GDP—but they may not. The easiest way to improve measured GDP evaluated using PPP exchange rates is, however, to implement policies that force people into the labor market and drive down wages (and thus prices for the rich). Such policies are good for measured GDP ... but catastrophic for society.

'Freedom,' 'democracy,' and 'corruption'

The richest countries in the world—richest in terms of GDP per capita—also happen to be the 'freest' countries in the world, the most 'democratic,' and the least 'corrupt.' Of course, it is the same countries that formerly defined 'rich' in terms of GDP per capita that have latterly defined freedom as the absence of any constraints on an individual's ability to acquire and control, democracy as the holding of regular elections in which candidates can spend unlimited amounts of money in self-promotion, and corruption as the perception of international businesspeople of the obstructions they face in doing business.

The standard measure of freedom in the world is an index published in the annual *Freedom in the world* report from the shadowy US advocacy organization, Freedom House, that, although technically an NGO, is reputed to be funded mainly by the US government. It does not release detailed budget figures, but the three largest contributors to its budget are two US government agencies and a UN agency that is mostly funded by the US government. According to its own website, it was founded in 1941 to combat Nazism, but five years later 'took up

—

the struggle against the other great twentieth century totalitarian threat, Communism.'

Every year Freedom House rates most of the countries of the world on a scale ranging from 1 ('free') to 7 ('not free'). The US (no surprise) consistently scores a 1. Perceived enemies of the US tend to do very poorly (Venezuela 5, Iran 6, Cuba 6.5) but so do many transparently unfree US allies (Uganda 4.5, Qatar 5.5, Afghanistan 6). Even a casual observer might question the characterization of Venezuela as less free than Uganda, but freedom after all is in the eye of the beholder, and in this case, the beholder is a Washington-based NGO primarily funded by the US government.

In the case of the Freedom House index, freedom literally is in the eye of the beholder—each country currently receives in-house 'expert' ratings on each of 10 political rights questions and 15 civil liberties questions. How its 18 mainly young, mainly US in-house experts are able to judge in detail the political landscapes of 195 countries every year is a bit of a mystery, but to be fair to Freedom House, it doesn't claim that its statistics are definitive. It's just that with no one else having the arrogance to publish annual freedom measures for 195 countries, Freedom House is the only game in town.

Freedom House also defines countries as being 'electoral democracies' (there are 117 of these) or not (78), but at least here it has some competition. An independent (US) academic group, the Polity IV Project, rates the level of democracy for 164 countries. Polity IV scores may not be as obviously biased as Freedom House scores, but they are still based on a very US conceptualization of democracy as a process involving competitive elections. Neither Freedom House nor Polity IV nor any other widely available set of political statistics seems capable of conceiving of democracy as meaning anything other than competitive elections.

When it comes to competitiveness, US (national) elections are unparalleled in the world. But is that all democracy means? The US electoral process at all levels has been a duopoly of the same two major parties since 1864, punctuated by the occasional self-funded maverick millionaire candidate. Corporations can spend unlimited amounts of money to lobby politicians in their favour, and politicians can and do routinely resign office to take up multi-million dollar positions lobbying for the very industries they formerly directly regulated. If this is democracy, the word has little meaning beyond its technical definition as a system of competitive elections.

It is in the measurement of corruption, however, that rich country hypocrisy takes the cake. The rich countries of the world have created an anti-corruption watchdog NGO, Transparency International (TI), that is 85 per cent funded by rich country governments (with most of the rest coming from the Bill & Melinda Gates Foundation). The organization has used its Corruption Perceptions Index (CPI) to effectively define corruption in global political discourse in terms of large corporations' perceptions and Western experts' opinions of how corrupt a country is.

As a result, in a country where companies can win multi-billion dollar contracts by hiring former government officials to conduct intensive government lobbying (such as the US or UK), the sources behind the CPI find no corruption. On the other hand, a country where a police officer might solicit a US$10 bribe to waive a speeding ticket is considered highly corrupt. Countries that are particularly unfriendly to multinational corporations are found to be the most 'corrupt' of all. Venezuela, for example, is ranked as the 10th most corrupt country in the world, tied with Equatorial Guinea. Venezuela may be many bad things, even corrupt, but it beggars belief to suggest that Venezuela is one of the most corrupt places on Earth.

Hungarian sociologist Endre Sik has flatly stated: 'I consider the Corruption Perceptions Index (CPI) to be the worst among the existing corruption-perception techniques,' but the others are no better. In fact, the CPI includes 14 other such indices in its construction. The real corruption is in the definition of corruption itself. The CPI claims to measure 'the misuse of public power for private gain.' It does not, however, consider the private capture of public power to be corruption. The official who solicits a bribe is corrupt; the executive who bribes an official is not. With no

---

apology for the corrupt official, most large-scale corruption emanates from the private sector. But that is development: government in the service of business.

Government in the service of the people is ... 'dangerous.'

Recommended reading

Costanza, R., Hart, M., Posner, S. and Talberth, J. (2009) *Beyond GDP: The need for new measures of progress*, Boston, MA: Boston University, The Frederick S. Pardee Center for the Study of the Longer-Range Future.

Galtung, F. (2006) 'Measuring the immeasurable: Boundaries and functions of (macro) corruption indices,' in C. Stampford, A. Shacklock, C. Connors and F. Galtung (eds) *Measuring corruption*, Aldershot: Ashgate Publishing, pp 101-30.

Galtung, J. (1969) 'Violence, peace, and peace research,' *Journal of Peace Research*, vol 6, no 3, pp 167-91.

Ilcan, S. and Phillips, L. (2010) 'Developmentalities and calculative practices: The Millennium Development Goals,' *Antipode*, vol 42, no 4, pp 844-74.

Korzeniewicz, R.P., Stach, A., Patil, V. and Moran, T.P. (2004) 'Measuring national income: A critical assessment,' *Comparative Studies in Society and History*, vol 46, no 3, pp 535-86.

Kotkin, S. and Sajó, A. (2002) *Political corruption in transition: A skeptic's handbook*, Budapest: Central European University Press.

Kuznets, S. (1941) *National income and its composition, 1919-1938*, New York: National Bureau of Economic Research.

Maddison, A. (1995) *Monitoring the world economy, 1820-1992*, Paris: OECD Development Centre.

Munck, G.L. and Verkuilen, J. (2002) 'Conceptualizing and measuring democracy—Evaluating alternative indices,' *Comparative Political Studies*, vol 35, no 1, pp 5-34.

Stiglitz, J.E., Sen, A. and Fitoussi, J.-P. (2010) *Mismeasuring our lives: Why GDP doesn't add up*, New York: The New Press.

Sumner, A. (2007) 'Meaning versus measurement: Why do "economic" indicators of poverty still predominate?' *Development in Practice*, vol 17, no 1, pp 4-13.

Vanoli, A. (2005) *A history of national accounting*, Amsterdam: IOS Press.

—

THREE

Alternatives to the cult of growth

The Mexican polymath and social critic José María Sbert knew everything you could want to know about progress. His brilliant mind, his amazing erudition on this central myth of Western civilization, and his sensitivity for all things human allowed us to see, with him, that this secular idol of the modern era, moving and controlling it, is now ripe for the museum. A few years before his untimely death in 2006 he gave new use to the expression supposedly coined by Napoleon, 'the yellow danger.' He was not so concerned with China's military power as with its development, the contemporary face of progress.

After 1948 there was the impression that China would be able to find its own path, always on the verge of the abyss but not falling into it (and thus accelerating the fall of the world), Sbert mused. Bicycles inspired his hope. But then development came. What to do, Sbert asked, when there are 100 million Chinese people who own cars and will not allow for the circulation of 700 million bicycles? In the biggest cities, where a few cars were once forced to navigate six-lane avenues filled with a sea of bicycles, bicycles are now forced off the street and onto the pavements. Sbert's nightmare is already reality.

Sbert discovered that some Chinese people, perhaps many, have been thinking that the best thing that could happen to China would be to bang its head against a brick wall. He quoted the Under-Secretary of Environment of the Chinese government, in an interview for *Der Spiegel* in 2006, who observed that "our cities grow, but also our deserts; usable and habitable land had reduced to a half in the last 50 years," and then expressed the hope that

—

"the miraculous economic growth of China will stop because the environment will not be able to sustain it.... To believe that economic prosperity will automatically bring political stability is a great mistake.... If the chasm between rich and poor becomes bigger, the country and the society will be destabilized."

China has not been able to build a **harmonious society**, the goal of its 11th five-year plan (2006-10). The society is already suffering instability. Every year at least 80,000 mass protests erupt in the country. For Sbert, to imagine 1.5 billion Chinese people (the projected number for 2020) living the American way of life, with the same per capita consumption of energy, with the same passion for consumerism, with the family car and a thousand gadgets, was another name for the apocalypse. An increasing number of people are currently dreaming such a nightmare.

In spite of the so-called financial crisis, the worst financial crisis in the history of capitalism, which for Wallerstein and others would be in its terminal phase, the development enterprise seems to be in full-fledged development. International institutions and politicians insist that corporations should be allowed to do their job: creating jobs, because governments cannot or should not assume that responsibility. At the same time, the basic needs of everyone should be satisfied, extreme poverty eliminated, the MDGs achieved ... no fact, no experience, no argument seems enough to create a crack in this dominant mentality. China is still the star of the BRICs, as along with Brazil, Russia, and India they are leading all other 'developing' countries on the path to reduced poverty and the good life, the good American life.

But cracks, profound cracks, are now evident in this way of thinking. The mood that in the 1980s made it possible to seriously discuss postdevelopment is now shaping the attitudes of millions at the grassroots level, all over the world. More and more people are beginning to see the nakedness of the emperor.

NAFTA and the Zapatista revolt

At midnight, on 1 January 1994, NAFTA (the *North America Free Trade Agreement* between Mexico, the US, and Canada) came into force. Mexico, according to its President, was on the verge of becoming a member of the first world, the global North. Barely two hours later, thousands of Indians, in a strikingly well-organized operation, armed with machetes, clubs, and a few guns, occupied seven of the main towns in Chiapas, a province on Mexico's southern border with Guatemala. Two dozen police officers and an unknown number of rebels died in the first skirmishes.

During the tense calm that followed, they showed notable respect for people and property (with the exception of government buildings), and announced their intentions. They called themselves the *Ejército Zapatista de Liberación Nacional* (EZLN, Zapatista Army for National Liberation). Their rebellion against the President and the national army was also against 500 years of oppression and 40 years of 'development.' Their motto: ¡Basta! Enough!

The following day, Mexican President Carlos Salinas launched a massive attack on the rebels using French tanks, Swiss airplanes, US helicopters, and 15,000 troops. Nobody knows the full extent of the violence that followed, but there were reports of civilian killings, torture, summary executions, and unlawful detentions. Salinas dismissed the uprising as the work of "a local group of professionals of violence, probably foreigners."

The ideological slant of EZLN's declarations was puzzling. A guerrilla movement struggling for democracy, with no aspirations to seize formal power? An Indian movement not showing ethnic fundamentalism—but opposing NAFTA? A movement of illiterate peasants talking about transnational capital and using electronic networks to gain support for their struggle? Within days of the rebellion, millions came out in support, not necessarily of the rebels' violent actions, but of their demands for freedom, justice, and democracy.

Mounting opposition at home and abroad forced the government to change course. The President called a ceasefire and amnesty and made a

—

51

number of political concessions. These included—of course—the promise of money to everyone in Chiapas, particularly the rebels. The President also appointed a personal Commissioner for Peace and Reconciliation. The EZLN accepted the dialogue with the Commissioner, under its own conditions. It started in February and ended two months later, when the EZLN said 'No' to the government's main offer to the Indians, development, as a substitute for what they wanted, justice, freedom, and democracy.

The end of the illusion

Truman effectively spoiled development by using 200 years of the social construction of a complex concept for his limited purposes. There is no way out of the political shape he gave to the word. The time has come to recognize that the concept itself is dead, and to stop the search for new emblems to revive it.

For the social majorities, development was always a threat, but it came accompanied by promises of continual improvement. They reacted with ambivalence: they resisted a process that endangered their very subsistence and destroyed their environments, while hoping to be included in what looked like an epic adventure and the way to a better life.

In the 1980s, however, a new generation of experts documented what many people already knew: the damages done by the development experiment. Radical thinkers lucidly articulated a new awareness, emerging from experiences that transformed the weakening of public and private developers into an opportunity for new initiatives. Instead of further resistance or claims, a new ethos beyond development appeared.

The new awareness of the 1980s 'lost decade' for development, that the 'underdeveloped' were not catching up and that instead of levelling social hierarchies development was bringing more injustice into the world, produced rage and frustration in millions of people. But it also nourished a new hope. As the Indians from the south of Mexico firmly expressed at the beginning of 1994, the time had come to say 'Enough!'

During the 18th Conference of the Society for International Development, held in Rome on 1-4 July 1985, in a panel about the future of development studies, one of the panelists suggested that scholars focus on the archaeology of the field. That panelist was Gustavo Esteva. Only an archaeological eye, he argued, would be able to explore the ruins left by development. Like many others, he was no longer seeing development in the present and even less in the future, but rather in the past.

In fact, by 1985 the growing frustration with the pains and failures of development opened minds to the suggestion that there would not be a fourth development decade. Even the cynicism of international bureaucrats had a limit. The age of postdevelopment was poised to 'take off.' Gilbert Rist formulated this beautifully: "A mere restoration of the ancient past—whatever the glory attached to it in collective memories— was out of question. But a forward run in the present path of development was equally absurd."

Ivan Illich invited some of his friends to begin a conversation on "After development, what?" Gathered in 1985 in his house in Ocotepec, Mexico, they first tried to describe in one word what they were seeing. The image that came immediately to the mind of one of them was hospitality: to escape from development implied first of all to leave behind a view of the world that could not recognize the otherness of the other. After centuries of intolerance, Western society became tolerant. Tolerance, however, is but the most civil form of intolerance. To tolerate, states the dictionary, is to suffer with patience. To tolerate conveys an implicit rejection of the condition of the other. To tolerate is, in fact, to insult, said Goethe. The social majorities are coming to the point in which they can no longer tolerate the tolerance or the intolerance they have suffered for more than 500 years. They cannot accept less than hospitality.

The conversation continued in Puerto Rico, where they modified the expression "After development, what?"—too evolutionist, too developmentalist—to ask instead "Beyond development, what?" After three years of conversation in different countries, "in the fall of 1988, sitting on the porch of Barbara

—

Duden's wooden house at State College in Pennsylvania," the group felt that the moment had come to share with others the outcome of the conversation. "After an intense week of debate interrupted by cutting onions and uncorking bottles," they drew up the plan for a book, and Wolfgang Sachs accepted the mandate to become its editor.

It was easy to come to agreement on the form of the book they were imagining. They knew that development occupied the center of an incredibly powerful semantic constellation. At the same time, they knew that very few words were as feeble, as fragile, and as incapable of giving substance and meaning to thought and behaviour. The key concepts of the development discourse are like the buoys of a net. Within the net, you are trapped by what you catch. You cannot open yourself to the open sea. It is a net that operates as a prison. The essays of those participating in the conversation would be the entries of a dictionary, *The development dictionary: A guide to knowledge as power*, "to expose some of the unconscious structures that set boundaries on the thinking of our epoch." The book was "an invitation to review the developmental model of reality and to recognize that we all wear not merely tinted, but tainted, glasses if we take part in the prevailing development discourse."

"The vision of a world integrated under the rule of reason and welfare was carried by a view of history which today is rapidly becoming ripe for the museum," Sachs wrote in his contribution. Universalism is under siege. Globalization is no substitute for it. It has become increasingly impossible to think, "that the coherence of the world can be achieved by pushing ahead along a common path towards some distant promised future. Coexistence has to be sought in the context of the present."

In Truman's time, the promise of development presented the American way of life as a universal ideal, an illusion then capable of capturing the imagination of the world. Movies were the new entertainment and Hollywood presented such a way of life as closest to paradise. But this fantasy was dismantled, step-by-step, in the following years. The ideal is not universalizable: all sorts of limits, among which the environmental ones are increasingly

—

included, prevent it. And the ideal itself is open to criticism: it is not an attractive model for everyone, and many of its traits seem increasingly inappropriate.

To extend its attraction of the ideal, to forestall gathering criticisms, development goals got a more sensible appearance. They focused, for example, on the basic needs approach, or on attaining minimum acceptable *standards of living*. This trend is evident today in the MDGs. The alleviation of poverty and hunger became the chief priority of development. But the universal nature of the enterprise was never abandoned. Greening it, giving it a human face, or adding slogans such as participation or self-help did not eliminate its illusory and ethnocentric nature—nor its colonial stamp.

Different peoples and cultures define in different ways what living well is. They freely determine, in their own terms, what they need. Once people dream again their own dreams, and trust their own noses—more than the expert's—developers peddling universal 'basic' needs can no longer deceive them. Free people claim, through concrete behaviours, the right to choose their own way. An increasing number of people, among those many still called 'underdeveloped' or 'developing,' are saying 'no thanks' to such redefinitions of human nature. For them, the ability to feel well is not defined as the right of access to particular medical services; the ability to learn what is needed, to get social recognition for what one knows, and to ensure cultural continuity from one generation to the next, is not associated with the hanging of a school diploma; the ability to settle and dwell in a meaningful space, modifying the environment according to one's cultural patterns, and rooting oneself in a commons in which virtue is possible, is not associated with the right to housing and urban services.

The new attitude in many social movements is to abandon conventional universalism without falling into cultural relativism. It expresses in practice, based on local traditions and ancient experiences of resistance and liberation, what Raimón Panikkar has conceptualized as **radical pluralism**. This position acknowledges the existence of human invariants, but not cultural

—

universals. In accepting cultural diversity as a precondition for harmony among peoples and recognizing that no person may represent the totality of human experience, cultural relativity (not relativism) is assumed, which means that every view of the world is relative to its context and no one can hold a complete and absolute view of reality.

It does not seem feasible to incorporate radical pluralism into the design of the nation-state, formally based on a pact of homogeneous individuals, designed around the notion of full **sovereignty** over all of them and based on violence and the universal application of juridical norms. Recent constitutional reforms in countries such as Bolivia, Ecuador, and Mexico are advances in the right direction, recognizing the existence of **indigenous** peoples, but making evident the limits of their autonomy: the very design of the nation-state does not allow for **juridical pluralism**.

If indigenous nations and people don't often articulate such demands in public, it is because they know from bitter experience how harshly colonizing states react to such declarations.

For example, the Mexican government did not honour its commitment in the Accords of San Andrés with the Zapatistas for a constitutional reform recognizing the indigenous peoples of Mexico and their rights to autonomy and self-determination. The government and the political parties began to speak of 'balkanization' and swung into counter-reform before the reforms were ever carried out. The Zapatistas have been implementing the Accords in their own territory, demonstrating that instead of division and conflict, **people's sovereignty** means peaceful and harmonious coexistence of the different, through juridical pluralism and political autonomy. They had never been separatists—they want to materialize their dreams in Mexico. But as the National Indian Congress states, "Never again a Mexico without us."

A future of full sovereignty is very unlikely for any of today's indigenous populations. Most have accordingly moderated their demands to mere claims to requests for juridical pluralism. Even these are rarely taken seriously by the institutions of settler states. Quite the contrary: whatever their other differences, the world's existing states show incredible solidarity when it comes to the issue of plural sovereignty. In 2007, without ever formally defining indigeneity, the UN promulgated the UN Declaration on the Rights of Indigenous Peoples. Something of a final word on indigenous rights, its final article states flatly that:

> Nothing in this Declaration may be interpreted as ... construed as authorizing or encouraging any action which would dismember or impair, totally or in part, the territorial integrity or political unity of sovereign and independent States.

In other words: no sovereignty. Not even in the shape of people's sovereignty or mere expression of freedom.

In 1997, one of the authors of this book (Esteva) was an invited guest at an event held at the Intercultural Institute of Montreal. He observed that after six hours of patient and gentle conversation, a Canadian officer told a Mohawk Chief: 'You need to acknowledge that the Canadian government will never recognize the sovereignty of the Mohawk people.' 'We are not interested,' firmly answered the Mohawk Chief. 'What you call sovereignty implies doing terrible things to Mother Earth and putting signs of no trespass. For the Mohawk, to be sovereign is to be free like the wind. That is what we want.' And this, not another nation-state separated from Canada, as sovereignty is usually interpreted, is what the Canadian government cannot accept.

Something similar happens with the questions of collective rights, those of 'minorities' or indigenous peoples. The nation-state may accept classifications of individuals in order to grant them special rights: workers, women, children, and so on. In the same way, it may grant special rights to the individual members of 'minorities:' tribes, peoples, ethnic groups, and so on. What it cannot incorporate is the very idea of collective rights, the rights of a collectivity that is something more than and distinct from the individuals constituting it. Many indigenous peoples, as well as other 'minorities,' have successfully created de facto institutional arrangements expressing the reality of their collective will and existence, usually at odds with the governments of the countries within which they exist. It is increasingly clear that they conceive their reality within a new political and epistemological paradigm that the nation-state cannot accommodate.

The design of the nation-state, the ideal arena for the creation and expansion of capitalism, has become an obstacle in the era of globalization. It is not clear what kind of political design will replace it, but whatever it is would have to include the principles of juridical pluralism. For many of those still considered as objects of development, the ideals of this era are entirely depleted. They may fall again into old illusions, due to the fascination they still feel for some fruits of modernity, but the latter is no longer an obstacle to their putting their own definitions of what living well is at the center of their dreams and their daily efforts. They are already living in a new era.

Indigeneity and the nation-state in Australia

In 1972 a group of aboriginal activists in Australia established an 'embassy' on the lawn of Australia's Parliament House. Despite repeated harassment and attacks, it has been in existence in some form or another ever since. The activists demanded no less than to be recognized as the representatives of sovereign nations (there are many aboriginal nations in Australia). They did not think of themselves as human rights activists advocating for fair treatment of a minority; they considered themselves delegates acting in the name of sovereign peoples.

The Federation of Aboriginal Sovereign Nations celebrated 40 years of the tent embassy on 26 January 2012. 26 January, 'Australia Day' to the Australian state and the majority of the citizens of Australia, is known to many aboriginal residents of Australia as 'Sovereignty Day,' a commemoration of the day the UK declared white settler sovereignty over the continent that was to become known as Australia. Since that day in 1788 the indigenous inhabitants of Australia (known in Australia as aboriginal people) have been progressively corralled into small rural settlements or marginalized as an urban underclass.

Of course, the indigenous nations of Australia are not alone in having been corralled and marginalized. In many places (as in Tasmania in Australia) indigenous nations have been entirely exterminated. In others they have been forcibly expelled (as in the infamous 'Trail of Tears' by which the indigenous nations of the southeastern US were expelled to what is now Oklahoma). In many cases indigenous nations have been demographically swamped by land-hungry settler nations (as in India, in much of the Arctic Circle, and in today's Tibet). In much of Latin America indigenous nations constitute local or national majorities that are nonetheless subjugated by European-heritage ruling classes.

Australian indigenous activists are not alone in calling for sovereignty—for recognition as a nation. The aboriginal tent embassy delegates demanded one step less than full sovereignty: they demanded a state within Australia in what is now the Northern Territory, similar to the limited sovereignty that Canadian first peoples have now achieved in the Canadian Arctic province of Nunavut. In Norway the Sami nation has its own parliament with limited jurisdiction over Sami affairs (although without the power to legislate). In the US many Indian nations enjoy a more limited sovereignty over tribal lands and institutions, although most demand further rights. The Iroquois nations of North America have issued passports since at least the 1920s and compete in international sports as a separate nation, often in the face of severe opposition.

The underlying demand of many indigenous nations, however, is for sovereignty: for recognition of their status as independent states with full control over their own land, language, and laws. Imagine a sovereign aboriginal state in the center of Australia, avoiding all the main settler population centers but controlling nearly all of Australia's natural resources. With half a million people but five million square kilometres of land, such a state would be rich on the scale of Kuwait or Brunei. It is hard to imagine that such a rich country would find itself with a life expectancy of just 62 years, a 50 per cent smoking rate, a 57 per cent obesity rate, a high prevalence of gasoline sniffing among children, and over 40 per cent of all young males arrested *in any given year*—as reported in Australian Bureau of Statistics data for indigenous Australians. The indigenous populations of most other settler countries exhibit similarly poor statistics. Their statistical profiles are consistent with their social statuses as people living under foreign occupation.

The right to stop development

International bureaucracies build on what they have built before. In 1992 the preparatory committee for the United Nations Conference on Environment and Development (UNCED) rightfully invoked, for the *Earth Declaration*, the Stockholm Conference of 1972. The Stockholm Conference had captured the ecological concerns of the times, although it produced nothing more than the usual bureaucratic expansion, a new organ of the UN (the UN Environment Programme, or UNEP). The preparatory committee could just as well have invoked the 1970 International Strategy for Development, which urged governments "to arrest the deterioration of the human environment and to take measures towards its improvement, and to promote activities that will help maintain the ecological balance on which human survival depends." Even better would have been to invoke the Rome Club's *Limits to growth* report, Cocoyoc's notion of "environmental protection" (1974), the "ecologically appropriate change" perspective of the Hammarskjöld Foundation (1975), the "balanced ecodevelopment" of RIO (Reshaping the International Order, 1976), or even the maximum ceiling for industrial consumption of the Netherlands Symposium on the **New International Economic Order** (1975).

But the preparatory committee looked in other archives: it mined in more glorious episodes, where development was universally praised. The rhetoric used in the Earth Declaration draft tried to forget the lessons of the 1970s and to bring back the power games, rather than the environmental concerns, of that decade. The governments of Southern countries that used the oil shocks of the 1970s to argue for greater conservation seemed to believe that ecology might give them an ace in the hole to get the flow of resources they dreamed of. They did not

—

get much more than a declaration. And they paid the price of missing the opportunity to overcome the prejudices preventing everyone everywhere from seriously coping with the injustices of environmental devastation.

The governments of the 'underdeveloped' countries wanted to 'develop:' to be like the 'developed' are, to have what they have, while recognizing that such a goal is as unfeasible as it is irrational. Their contention—supported by the newly emerging economic orthodoxy—was that development is endogenous and depends on internal social change, but they clung to the international context to claim for help from the rich countries. President Marcos of the Philippines expressed this position in the name of the Group of 77 countries: "If the rich countries do not intervene to foster the growth of the underdeveloped countries, they must not hope to get rid of the burden of those not being helped by them" (Nairobi, 1976). The call to the rich in 1992, this time in the name of the environment, and the implicit blackmail, was equally equivocal: if the rich do not help the poor to fight poverty and underdevelopment, the poor will continue the destruction of the remaining natural resources of the world.

Development offered the utopia that all countries may have access to the American way of life. So Truman promised. Everybody believed it: Nehru and Stalin, Nasser and Willy Brandt. **Sustainable development** attempted to renovate the utopia, hiding the contradictions and consecrating the illusion. If it could be accomplished, the Americanization of the world would be an indescribable ecological catastrophe: Sbert's nightmare. Development and environmental protection are incompatible.

If you live in Rio or Mexico City today, you need to be very rich or very numb to fail to notice that development stinks. To hide such smells of development, every kind of deodorant has been applied: 'integral,' 'social,' 'endogenous,' 'human,' 'participatory,' 'sustainable' development. Development promises cultural enrichment while wiping out whole cultures to implant its global monoculture. If the real issue is to sustain nature and

—

culture, not development, if what matters is to respect peoples, in all their diversity, and to propitiate their flourishing and enduring, if the point is to allow for the highly varied forms of being in the world to exist and affirm themselves in their plurality, thus allowing them to care for their natural and cultural environments, we need to say 'no' to development in the form it is offered by the global North and accepted by the elites of the global South.

And that is precisely what the social majorities are asking for—and doing.

We live in peculiar times, forcing us to find answers in the past because we cannot find them in the present and even less in an increasingly uncertain future. We need to look back. The past may be a source of inspiration or an unbearable burden. People in villages and *barrios* are finding in their traditions inspiration to sensibly and wisely cope with their present predicaments, fully aware that one of their best traditions is the tradition of changing traditions in the traditional way, a trick that allows them to adapt continually to new circumstances without betraying themselves. International bureaucrats have instead been stirring their files, only to retrieve from the wastebasket battered emblems that continue to paralyze their imaginations; they may perhaps extend the agony of the myths still nourishing their budgets, but they will fail to cope with the present challenges.

Given the clamour for justice and ecological good sense that provoked the Earth Summit in 1992, the right that should have been approved was the right to stop development. What was approved, instead, was a kind of *Pax Americana*: a permanent state of war against the social majorities—and the environment—in the name of development, a war against people's autonomous subsistence, sacrificing it on the altar of an illusion.

Redevelopment and the rise of neoliberalism

From the very beginning, the 1980s looked like the 'lost decade for development' that they finally turned out to be. The public perception of development became highly unstable and volatile. The failures of the earlier declared **development decades** were widely recognized by scholars, politicians, and practitioners. Even as many of them began to cook up new development strategies, a mood beyond development appeared among others. A burgeoning literature documented the theoretical and practical search for alternatives to development, while the still dominant discourse on development options became a tiring and boring exercise in tautology, the end of the road, a dead end.

All these reflections reflected the turbulence of the times. New dreams began to be dreamt to escape from the nightmare of the 1980s, especially in Latin America and Africa, but throughout the rest of the world as well. The economic crises of the 1980s freed common men and women all over the world to rediscover the strength, richness, and vitality of their own political ventures and movements, well rooted in their traditions. They started to shake off or even dismantle the different oppressive political regimes, in both North and South, with astounding sociological imagination and political vigour. One after the other, dozens of government regimes were dismantled or reshaped: from the more despotic, entrenched, rigid, and dinosauric regimes, such as those in Romania and Chile, to the more flexible, 'modern,' 'democratic,' and 'progressive,' such as those in India or Hungary. Even the nominally Communist reactionary leaders of China came close to being toppled in 1989.

At the same time, too many people's initiatives revealed severe limitations. They displayed a tragic inability to get rid of the obsessions of development and a dramatic lack of interest or skill to translate their micro experiences into alternative macro designs to oppose the prevailing ones. At the very edge of the deep, radical departure embedded or explicitly expressed by their initiatives, they seemed to stop short, step back, and let old views and political styles prevail again. The political vacuum left by these limitations was immediately occupied by yet another wave of developers, ready to give development another lease of life.

And so, instead of being the burial decade of a dead myth, the 1980s propped up and cosmeticized the corpse. The 1990s ushered in the era of **redevelopment**, propelled along two

—

clearly distinguishable lines that have shaped the world we live in today.

In the North, redevelopment was needed to correct the maldevelopment of the post–Second World War period in which all the efforts of the capitalist West had to be directed against the Communist menace from the East. Europe had to open its labor markets. The US had to open its trade flows. Japan had to reform its government bureaucracy. In all cases, what seemed to be required was to redevelop, that is, to develop again what was maldeveloped or had become obsolete. In the US and the former Soviet Union, in Spain as in Switzerland, Austria, Poland, and England, public attention was called to the speed and conditions under which what was previously developed (socialized medicine, nuclear plants, steel production, pre-microchip manufacturing, polluting factories, or poisonous pesticides) must be destroyed, dismantled, exported, or substituted. The good, the bad, and the ugly: the whole postwar social model was to be discarded to make way for **neoliberalism**.

In the South, redevelopment took on a different meaning. It also meant dismantling or destroying what was still left over from the IMF-mandated **structural adjustment** processes of the 1980s in order to make room for the latest hand-me-downs imported from the North (nuclear waste, obsolete or polluting plants, unsellable or illicit commodities) and for the *maquiladoras* (those fragmented and provisional pseudofactories that the North would keep in operation during the transitional period), as well as for ultra-modern **enclaves** dutifully transnationalized. The obsession with remaining competitive, the fear of being left out of the race, encouraged the displacement and destruction of complete sections of what had been developed in the previous development decades. The emphasis of redevelopment in the South was associated with the economic recolonization of the **informal sector** and reliance on foreign **remittances** by migrants for basic subsistence. In the name of modernization and under the banner of poverty wars, redevelopment launched the last and definitive assault against both passive and organized resistance to development.

—

The recolonization of the South—and increasingly today the internal colonization of parts of the North—has led to the rise of a global **precariat**. The precariat is a precarious proletariat, similar to what Marx called the lumpenproletariat, with the difference that Marx considered the lumpenproletariat a deviant, marginal state, whereas the precariat is the new normal embraced by the world's leading governments and developmentalist institutions. Members of the precariat have lost the standard labor conditions they previously enjoyed: a safe, stable job with appropriate access to education, health services, pension plans, holiday time, and so on. They are thus joining the ranks of the underdeveloped majority, even when they live in Birmingham or Chicago.

British economist Guy Standing and many other contemporary liberals advocate guaranteed basic minimum incomes to prevent people falling into the precariat. This is not a new idea. 'Basic needs' and other fashionable novelties of the 1970s have received a new lease of life from developers promising protection against the social short-sightedness of economic growth and the anti-populist or anti-statist measures defining the mortal spell of neoliberal globalization. The welfare state would not be entirely dismantled, as some enthusiastically announced and many feared. But the global neoliberal project was steadfastly implemented with no recognition of limits.

Today's development ethos, which emerged in the 1990s, follows the two clearly distinguishable lines mentioned above: redevelopment and structural adjustment. The new emblem of globalization has become the universal catechism of governments, political parties, and international institutions. The coalition of political and economic forces that gave birth to the WTO, the quintessential institution of our times, took for granted the leadership of the only remaining superpower. Celebrated as the end of history, or condemned as the tombstone of old dreams of emancipation, the new credo seemed to define the one and only path for the whole world in the 21st century: redevelopment now donning the latest, designer-made, green mantel of ecological fix-its.

—

The new private cities

Some economists have recently begun to entertain the idea of a highly controversial socioeconomic experiment. Economist Paul Romer argues that **charter cities** should become the long sought-after engines of economic growth in developing countries. In this model, a host country provides 'unpopulated' land to build a new city from scratch to be planned and administered by private companies, making up their own laws and tax systems.

The idea of creating business-friendly enclaves is derived from anomalous postcolonial enclaves such as Hong Kong and Singapore. A city designed on pro-business policies and intended as a gateway for international corporations is seen as the panacea to fast track economic development. Proponents argue that charter cities should have their own environmental regulations, immigration policies, and even police forces.

When the Honduran government announced plans in 2011 to develop a private city with Paul Romer as its principal consultant on the project, it sparked a frenzy of global media coverage, most of it focused either on grand hopes for the new city or the supposed short-sightedness of opponents who resisted the dispossession of indigenous land and the explicit corporatization of state functions.

The Honduran deal was the outcome of a US-supported coup in 2009, which installed a pro-business government. The idea for the charter city arose after the Chief of Staff to the new President, Octavio Sánchez, watched an online TED talk on the subject given by Paul Romer. Sánchez convinced his boss, President Porfirio Lobo, to support the initiative.

Lobo's charter city plans started to unravel almost as soon as they were announced. The first proposed city was situated on indigenous land guaranteed by treaty. The expected international investors proved hard to find. Then, in September 2012, Paul Romer himself resigned from the charter city oversight board. Finally, in October 2012, the Honduran Supreme Court had the courage to rule the plans unconstitutional in a near-unanimous 13-2 decision, despite the assassination of one of the plaintiffs' lead lawyers, indigenous rights activist Antonio Trejo-Cabrera.

—

Nonetheless, Romer claims to be undaunted by the defeat in Honduras and an earlier 2009 defeat in Madagascar, where the main charter city proponent, President Marc Ravalomanana, was overthrown in a military coup. Despite these failures, the international press remains in love with the idea of charter cities, with glowing reports appearing even in usually sceptical venues such as *The Guardian* and the BBC. Needless to say, the business press is solidly behind the idea.

Major concerns about charter cities include land seizure, violations of labor and civil rights, environmental risks, and breaches of national constitutions. A charter city strives to create a favorable environment for capital investors, but the broader effects on its citizens and the wider country are likely to be less favorable. As with any corporation, most of the profits from private cities will probably accrue to an elite few. A fair distribution of wealth within a charter city seems unlikely as it is planned to keep income taxes, corporate taxes, and value-added taxes low. Instead of benefiting the entire country, charter cities are designed to create huge profits for a minority while legally excluding the demands of the (poor) majority.

Beyond development

Buen vivir, expressing in Latin America a general reaction to these dominant trends, is usually complemented with mutual *crianza*, mutual nurturing. The 'sweet life,' the expression captured by Víctor Antonio Rodríguez Suy Suy in the north of Peru, is not a utopia, something to achieve, but the joy of the experience of having at hand what you need, within an austere way of life and great autonomy. In the sweet life farming is not a means for an end or a business, even though it may produce an income. What matters is the joy of the daily recreation (re-creation) of nature.

Quechua Indian activist Fernando Huanacuni repeatedly makes the point in his public statements that the horizon behind living well looks to reconstitute political, social, juridical, and economic power, but most of all, to reconstitute life itself, which has been severely damaged by Western projects. This generates all

—

sorts of tensions and contradictions with governments across the ideological spectrum, which tends to disqualify and criminalize these increasingly vigorous movements.

The ideology that transfers to governments and corporations responsibility for defining the good life belongs to a characteristically Western intellectual tradition: the construction of One World with different flags and pretexts. The Westernization of the world is the hidden agenda of development, under the assumption that the Western developed countries represent the culmination of human evolution guided by the arrow of progress. The arrow is currently broken and the idea of progress itself is tarnished. The cultural homogenization associated with the development enterprise finds increasing resistance everywhere. As the Zapatistas suggested in 1994, the time has come to celebrate the otherness of the other and to create a world in which many worlds can be hospitably embraced.

Instead of continuing to dissolve peoples and cultures, to integrate every man and woman on Earth into a universal and uniform design, the exploration of ways for the harmonious coexistence of the different should be the priority. This attitude points towards a political horizon beyond the nation-state, reformulates the democratic struggle and recovers autonomous definitions of living well emerging from autonomous centers for the production of knowledge. It challenges the dominant mood among governments, political parties, and experts, which is still obsessed with social engineering, trickle-down effects, and other beliefs of the old development religion.

Even governments openly opposed to mainstream paradigms, such as those of Bolivia, Ecuador, and Venezuela today, not to mention major independent powers such as China and India, still adopt the conventional catechism of development and repress as heretics grassroots movements that challenge it. But it is also true that resistance spreads. It has thus become possible to publicly debate a central precept of the dominant religion: the goal of accelerated economic growth. Fifty years of propaganda have converted the economists' dogma into a general prejudice. Without further discussion, accelerated economic growth is widely accepted as something desirable. An increasingly vigorous school of thinking and action, however, challenges this pernicious obsession and claims to abandon it.

To make sure that the economy and the population grow at the same pace appears to be a common-sense principle. But it is not. Many things should grow until they reach their correct proportion: plants, animals, people. If something continues to grow after reaching its correct size, the resulting protuberance may be called a cancer, an abnormal growth. Much of what increases when the formal economy continues to grow is a type of social cancer. Speculation grows, irrational or destructive production grows, corruption and waste grow, homicides grow, all at the cost of what really should increase: social justice and the wellbeing of the majority.

In every country there are things that have grown too much or that should be made smaller, and others that have not grown enough or that need to continue growing for the greater good. A high rate of economic growth, measured as usual through GDP, tends to reflect a growth in what is already large, a social cancer, and a diminishing of what should continue growing.

Economic growth produces the opposite of what it promises. It does not improve people's wellbeing, social justice, or the use of natural resources. Quite the opposite: it often generates poverty, inefficiency, injustice, and environmental destruction. There is an abundant historical record to support this argument. To mindlessly equate a high rate of economic growth as a social goal is pure nonsense. It can only be attributed to ignorance, cynicism, or a combination of the two.

In the early 1970s economist Paul Streeten rigorously documented for the International Labour Organization the perverse connection between economic growth and injustice. He demonstrated the association between greater growth and greater poverty, and the relation of cause and effect between one and the other. He also demonstrated the illusory and perverse nature of the famous 'trickle-down effect,' the idea that concentrated riches spill out onto the majority, generating wellbeing in their wake.

—

We need to recover a sense of proportion that is simply another form of common sense. To struggle against a culture of waste, disposability, destruction, and injustice, the culture that has produced global warming and the global diabetes epidemic, we can reclaim the sensible and responsible rejection of what is unnecessary. In the name of socially viable goals we can discard forever the idolatry of economic growth.

The advantages of a negative growth rate, clearly specifying what we would continue to stimulate, can today be presented as a reasonable social goal. For example, we might support the growth of highly efficient, productive, and sensible sectors, such as those that make up the majority of the persecuted 'informal' sector of household work, subsistence farming, and small tradespeople. This will imply a focus on strengthening the productive capacity of the majority, instead of supporting the inefficient giants of state or market monopolies. The economists' nightmare, a drop in GDP, could be a blessing for the majority.

It is time to stop the dominant insanity. Some things need to grow, and others need to contract. Our capacity to sustain ourselves and our vital autonomy should grow. Our expressions and spaces for exercising liberty and initiative should grow. The opportunities for living well should multiply, according to the way in which each individual and culture defines what it means to live well. And to make that possible, let us reduce the weight of a formal economy that oppresses us and wears us down, through everything that contradicts living well for everyone or destroys nature. That is what the ongoing insurrection is trying to achieve.

Hope from the margins

The development era is over. Nonetheless, evidence of the new era, appearing everywhere, is still perceived as an anomaly of the old. The old one, in turn, looks stronger than ever and the death it is carrying is still perceived as a symptom of vitality. If people are fooled by such images and are blind to the evidence of the new era, the economy will continue to dismantle and destruct its own creation to the point of collapse. An increasing number of people are currently aware that the survival of the human race and Planet Earth itself are at stake.

There are diverse options and alternative paths leading beyond the oppressive reign of *homo oeconomicus*. Common people are leading the way in walking down these footpaths, away from development's promises of salvation, towards options that offer genuine hope to the social majorities. A new hope is thus emerging from the margins. Common people had been seen for what they were not: not formal, not structured, not included in the national accounts; or they were seen for what they lacked: capital, entrepreneurship, work ethic, or education. That is, they were not seen. You cannot see what is not; you cannot see a lack.

But there they are, and they are more than ever, their ranks daily supplemented by workers dismissed from the increasingly casualized formal sector of the economy. Conventional wisdom perceives them as a threat, knocking at the doors of the industrialized world. Their 'silent invasion' is fostering discrimination, violence, and even racism. They are an immigration problem, a refugee problem, or a 'race' problem. But there are more of them every day. Harbingers of the death of the current system, they are bred by the system itself.

If it were possible to see them for the first time, finally recognizing that the 'other' exists and has the right to exist in dignity, on their own terms, it could become possible to perceive that they constitute a hope. Instead of new development plans, limits to development would be imposed. They would thus cope by themselves with their predicaments and cease to be a threat to those who consider themselves privileged. They also would contribute, through their modest examples, to the dissemination throughout the planet of more sensible and enduring ways of living, which have started to become attractive ideals even for those who postulated themselves for centuries as models for everyone.

Recommended reading

Apffel-Marglin, F., Bato, J.L., Berlan, J.-P., Bhai, N. and Bové, J. (2003) *Défaire le développement, refaire le monde*, Paris: Parangon.

Coronel, S. and Dixit, K. (2006) 'The development debate thirty years after *What now*,' in N. Hällström, O. Nordberg and R. Österbergh (eds) *Development dialogue—What next: Volume I: Setting the context*, Uppsala: Dag Hammarskjöld Foundation.

Esteva, G. (2010) 'From the bottom-up: New institutional arrangements in Latin America,' *Development*, vol 53, no 1, pp 64-9.

Hall, T.J. and Fenelon, J.V. (2009) *Indigenous peoples and globalization: Resistance and Revitalization*, Boulder: Paradigm Publishers.

Illich, I. (1971) *Celebration of awareness: A call for institutional revolution*, New York: Doubleday.

Illich, I. (1973) *Tools of conviviality*, New York: Harper & Row.

McMichael, P. (ed) (2009) *Contesting development: Critical struggles for social change*, New York: Routledge.

Panikkar, R. (1995) *Invisible harmony: Essays on contemplation and responsibility*, Minneapolis, MN: Fortress Press.

Rengifo, G. (2001) *Allin Kawsay: Concepciones de bienestar en el mundo andino amazónico*, Lima: PRATEC.

Rist, G. (2006) *The history of development: From western origins to global faith* (2nd edn), London: Zed Books.

Sachs, W. (ed) (2010) *The development dictionary: A guide to knowledge as power* (2nd edn), London: Zed Books.

Standing, G. (2011) *The precariat: The new dangerous class*, London: Bloomsbury Academic.

Streeten, P. (1980) 'The choices before us,' *Development*, vol 22, no 2/3, pp 3-9.

FOUR

There is enough for everyone

The UN Population Division (UNPD) projects the world's population to reach 9.7 billion by 2050. This is a nine-fold increase compared to the roughly one billion people who were competing over natural resources in the middle of the 18th century. Serious concerns have been raised about the threats of such a sheer population boost. One question has become particularly central to debates on population pressure: 'Is there enough for everyone?' Given the fact that current levels of consumption are exceeding the Earth's carrying capacity by far, this concern seems at first glance to be perfectly reasonable. The question, however, requires much more careful examination or, put differently, a profound 're-formulation.'

The **Malthusian** anxiety about overpopulation disseminated by the media in Europe and North America often seems (perhaps consciously) to overlook some important factors. Instead of bluntly asking if there is enough for everyone, it is probably much more reasonable to question current levels of consumption—in particular, in the global North. According to the World Resources Institute NGO, the richest 16 per cent of the world's population consume approximately 80 per cent of the planet's natural resources. Re-formulating the issue to embrace global inequalities of consumption would result in a much more holistic question—something along the lines of: 'How much is enough for everyone?'

Yet, the vast majority of academic and public discourse is narrowly concentrated on the threat of overpopulation and curbing population growth. In public debate, the alleged problem

—

73

of population growth is almost exclusively attributed to the global South. While in many Northern countries population numbers have started to decline due to low fertility rates, emigration, and birth control, most countries of the South see their population growing. In this respect, the countries that are attracting the most attention are China and India, with population growth rates between 1990 and 2010 of 17 and 40 per cent respectively (according to UNDP data). African countries are often thrown in for good measure—for Africa as a whole the population grew 61 per cent between 1990 and 2010.

It is important to note that even a complete halt to population growth would fail to stabilize current levels of natural resources consumption, simply because the problem is not increasing population, but increasing levels of gross overconsumption. Repercussions of unfettered consumption are evident in almost all social, economic, and ecological domains. To better understand how misleading the much-debated 'scarcity' actually is, one only needs to look at how consumption varies across developed and developing countries. What is scarce in poor countries is often available in abundance in rich countries. The key message here is not that the availability of food and natural resources cannot be sustained, but that their distribution cannot be sustained.

In this chapter, we discuss how resources and food scarcity are socially created rather than naturally given. The unpacking of food, water, resources, and 'atmospheric' scarcity makes clear that it is not the lack of natural resources *per se*, but the growing inequality of resource exploitation and distribution that undermine the opportunities of millions to satisfy their basic needs. We highlight the failure of Western development ideologies (pushing consumption, green growth, and efficiency) to curb the prevalence of undernourishment and starvation. We acknowledge that green-washing consumption will not suffice to free sufficient resources. Instead, we point out ways towards a new cultural narrative that calls for a departure from current growth ideologies. Such a paradigm shift may not only prove highly productive in curtailing global resource scarcity but also

—

in increasing subjective levels of wellbeing in both the North and South.

Thomas Malthus and population growth

Thomas Malthus (1766-1834) was a British economist who, in contrast to his contemporaries, believed that population growth was a threat to utopian society. Based on his observations that population growth occurred at a faster rate than increases in food production, he believed that famine and poverty were natural outcomes. In his *Essay on the principle of population* he proposed his famous theory on the causes and effects of overpopulation. His key argument was that while world population grew geometrically (1, 2, 4, 16, 32), food supply could only increase arithmetically (1, 2, 3, 4, 5). Therefore, a growing population would ultimately undermine the ability to feed itself once population growth had outstripped food production.

Notwithstanding, Malthus argued that in fact people would not go on to reproduce until they starved. He identified two different types of 'checks' that would slow down population growth and keep population from growing infinitely. *Preventative checks* included birth control, delayed marriage (moral restraint), restraint of procreation, and homosexuality, while *positive checks* resulted in premature deaths: diseases, war, and starvation. Malthus believed that the fear and emergence of famine would also prompt people to reduce birth rates.

Positive checks are said to result in a *Malthusian catastrophe* (also known as a *Malthusian check*, *Malthusian crisis* or *Malthusian disaster*). In the most extreme cases, catastrophes such as diseases, plagues, war, or starvation would revert humanity to subsistence agriculture. After population hit bottom, growth could then be restored. Malthus referred to these mechanisms as 'natural laws' and argued that once they were discovered, humankind would focus on preventative checks to balance population levels.

Unpacking ecological scarcity

Current population growth figures, combined with the latest ecological footprint data, draw a picture of serious global resource scarcity. Since at least the 1970s, the annual global consumption of natural resources has exceeded the sum of natural resources the Earth can reproduce each year. Put differently, current levels of consumption have surpassed the Earth's carrying capacity. To sustain current levels of consumption, humanity requires more than 1.5 planets, and in the long term, even more when taking into account globally rising levels of consumption. In public debate, excessive resource exploitation is commonly explained by and associated with population growth. The truth, however, is that natural resource scarcity is largely caused by the overconsumption of a minority, not by a majority which has comparatively low levels of per capita consumption.

One of the best ways to illustrate how the competition over natural resources is largely constructed is to look at humanity's ecological footprint data. The **ecological footprint** is an eco system-based indicator that measures the demand for natural resources, and provides information on whether or not countries are consuming beyond the planet's ecological carrying capacity. In a nutshell, the ecological footprint quantifies human pressure on the planet. By measuring the ecological footprint against the Earth's **biocapacity** we are able to answer two questions: 'Do we fit on the planet?' and 'Who is most responsible for the prevalence of resource scarcity?'

The ecological footprint is particularly useful for examining how resource scarcity is socially constructed rather than naturally given. This is technically feasible since the ecological footprint counts the natural resources used in the production of the goods and services consumed by a country. Thus, for example, the coal used to generate electricity in China to power toy factories that are producing toys for the US market is tallied against the American ecological footprint, not the Chinese one. This allows us to empirically assess how developed countries differ from developing countries in terms of natural resources consumption, independent of where the resources have been extracted and used.

According to ecological footprint data, global resource consumption is alarming. The world is not just heading towards an **ecological overshoot**, but has already passed it. According to the 2012 *Living planet* report from the World Wildlife Fund (WWF) conservation NGO, we are consuming an equivalent of 1.5 planets' worth of resources to provide the ecological resources necessary for the production, disposal, and absorption of the goods and services used today. Moderate UN estimates suggest that the equivalent of two Earths will be required by 2030 if current consumption trends continue.

A future rise in scarcity, however, cannot be simply attributed to the absolute lack of resources. The decisive factors are rather a highly unequal destruction and utilization of these resources. With regards to humanity's ecological footprint, it would take more than 4.5 planets if everyone lived like the average North American and only 1.6 planets if we were all to live like the average Brazilian. On the other hand, if everyone lived like the average person in India, less than half of the Earth's biological capacity would suffice to sustain the world's population.

Around the world, people in poorer countries are using significantly fewer resources than people in richer countries. According to the Global Footprint Network NGO the Earth has a biocapacity of 1.78 **global hectares** (gha) available to each citizen. Rich countries are running into massive ecological deficits (ecological footprints greater than 1.78), while many poor countries still operate within their ecological means (footprints smaller than 1.78). The former include countries such as the United Arab Emirates (UAE) (10.7 gha), the US (8.0 gha), and Canada (7.0 gha), while the latter comprise countries such as India (0.9), Indonesia (1.21), and Peru (1.5). Countries that exceed their ecological limits only slightly are, for example, China (2.2), Cuba (1.9), and Ecuador (1.9).

Cuba is a great counter-example to the prevailing notion that development requires a significant increase in natural resources use. The HDI places Cuba among those that enjoy high human

—

development and a high standard of living. The index ranks the country 50th out of 177. When plotting the HDI against ecological footprint data, it turns out that Cuba is one of the few countries with a relatively high standard of living that is close to operating within its ecological means. Contrary to the general notion that human development (HDI) and ecological deficit are inevitably correlated, Cuba demonstrates that a decoupling of living standards from material extraction is indeed possible.

Ecological footprint data reveals how different countries operate in terms of resource extraction and consumption. Most—if not all—rich countries have by far exceeded their fair resource shares. Massive economic growth and resource-intensive lifestyles have left many countries in an ecological debt that goes far beyond any tolerable level. Wrecking natural resources to sustain contemporary consumption levels in the North and to increase them in the South can only result in one thing: scarcity.

Unpacking food scarcity

According to estimates from the UN Food and Agriculture Organization (FAO), more than 25,000 people die every day of starvation or hunger-related causes. This is not due to some naturally given resource scarcity—there is plenty of food for everyone on this planet. We have to be very conscious about the fact that such an embarrassing catastrophic situation is entirely human made. People are not starving because of floods, droughts, crop failures, or water shortages. People are starving because a disproportionately large share of foodstuffs is extracted in the global South to be consumed (either as food, feedstuff, or biofuel) in the global North.

In his infamous book *Imperium der Schande*, Jean Ziegler speaks of the emergence of a neo-feudal empire that is "not able to nourish the world, but to enrich itself through the hunger in the world." He portrays the neo-emperors (*Kosmokraten*) to be primarily engaged in organising the scarcity of goods, services, and capital, resulting in the deaths of millions of people every year. Man-made scarcity results in food shortages and malnutrition,

—

making the hungry become weaker and thereby diminishing their chances to participate in the labor force. Without income, they become even hungrier and more vulnerable—a vicious cycle, almost impossible to break.

It has become increasingly popular to argue that there is not enough food for everyone, and overpopulation is often portrayed as the major problem here. This argument, however, has some serious weaknesses. The reasons why more than one billion people are hungry under the present global consumption model are manifold. Food scarcity is created through an array of complex mechanisms: rising meat demand in emerging economies, the increasing use of maize as a source for biofuel, increasing problems of water supply, unfavorable weather events (largely caused by climate change), transport costs, irrigation costs, and modern intensive food production methods. Meanwhile, Northern consumers have the economic capacity and moral impudence to afford the costs of thousands of air, sea, and truck miles to import out-of-season fruits and vegetables from the South.

While Western-style food consumption has led to alarming health problems such as obesity and diabetes, many countries in the South are still struggling to ensure food security. The UN FAO defines food security as a state "when all people, at all times, have physical, social and economic access to sufficient, safe and nutritious food that meets their dietary needs and food preferences for an active and healthy life." Despite significant advances in agricultural productivity, food security is still a very remote prospect for a large part of the world's population. While Northern levels of food consumption have long exceeded recommended dietary needs, many hungry in the South are still being expropriated from their fair share of food.

The global food crisis is in many ways also a global water crisis. The fact that more than 70 per cent of worldwide freshwater resources are used in agriculture shows that water is key to food security. Scarcity in water inevitably leads to scarcity in food. Research has shown that water-intensive Northern lifestyles have become one of the primary drivers of changes to the planet's

—

water systems. There are numerous examples of how the pursuit of greater consumption has demanded increased harnessing and supply of water. According to the NGO Global Compact, worldwide freshwater consumption has doubled since the end of the Second World War and is still rising rapidly. Nonetheless, a study from the Nature Conservancy NGO suggests that every year some 2.67 billion people experience some form of extended water scarcity.

Overconsumption of freshwater is primarily evident in three areas: agricultural, industrial, and domestic use. The amount of water withdrawal in each domain is typically correlated with a country's level of national income per capita. Richer countries tend to withdraw water primarily for industrial and domestic purposes while poorer countries withdraw most of the water for agriculture use. Thus, while poor countries use their water to feed people, rich countries use their water to support other, arguably less important, forms of consumption (for example, conspicuous consumption).

As with water, a closer look at the global patterns of food consumption debunks the convenient myth of natural scarcity and points to the highly unequal distribution of foodstuffs that is inherent in the global food chain. While the daily food intake of a typical European or North American exceeds by far what dieticians would recommend, undernourishment in many poor countries has been increasing steadily for the last decade. In 1996 the World Food Summit (WFS) settled on a quite moderate goal when the assembled heads of state and government urged the world to globally eradicate chronic hunger, achieve food security, and significantly reduce the number of undernourished people by 2015. A time frame of 19 years was proposed to half the number of undernourished people.

This goal will not be met. According to the UN FAO, the number of those undernourished increased from about 820 million in 1997 to over one billion in 2009. A dozen years after the WFS declaration, there were almost 200 million more hungry people in the world. At the same time, food consumption and food waste (the disposal of perfectly edible food) in the

North has exceeded all previous records. There is no moral or technological justification for the people of the North to consume and throw away enormous amounts of food rather than leaving more for the (actual) hungry. This is exactly the 'disgrace' that Jean Ziegler describes.

Another contributor to rising food prices, food shortages, and severe starvation in the South is the progressive globalization of food supply. Most notably, it is the insatiable taste for meat in developed countries that seriously affects food security in poor countries. The production of beef is particularly resource-intensive, requiring 15,000 litres of water per kilogramme (according to National Geographic Society's water footprint data). Meat production results in the clearing of forests (to make space for pasture land), carbon dioxide (CO_2) emissions (through transport miles and energy-intensive production), and methane (CH_4) emissions (through animal flatulence). But today meat is no longer a privilege of the rich. The global dissemination of Northern food culture has changed century-old dietary patterns of populations in which meat has never played any significant role. In China, for example, UN FAO figures show that per capita meat consumption increased from 3.8kg in 1961 to 52.4kg in 2002, reinforcing the pressure on global food prices and availability.

Another pitfall of Northern-style consumption is its infinite hunger for energy. **Biofuel** policies such as the EU's Renewable Energy Directive (RED) are pushing up food prices and reviving fears of food shortages. In this directive, the EU is planning a binding target that mandates that 10 per cent of transport fuels come from renewable sources by the end of 2020. Most recently, the EU has realized the danger of their proposed mandate and is currently discussing cutting the binding target in half. Under such policies, arable land is increasingly being transformed into monocultures exclusively reserved for the production of biofuels. Every hectare gained for the production of biofuel is removed from the production for actual (edible) food. Land that had for centuries been used for food production is now reserved for growing stocks to match the growing demands of energy-

—

intensive lifestyles. Also, large parts of the world's few remaining rainforests are being cut down to give way to the production of fuel stocks.

The current Northern economic model has made its priorities very clear: biofuel production over food security. On the world market the prices for biofuels are higher than for foodstuffs that makes it tempting for farmers to change to biofuel production instead of continuing to grow actual food. This quest for profit results in food scarcity and an increase in food prices for the hungry. Again, food scarcity is seen to be the result not of natural limits, but of socially constructed policy decisions made in the interests of corporate profit and energy-intensive consumerism.

Unpacking atmospheric scarcity

The competition over natural resources also extends to emission activities. Here, the message is: 'There is not enough air for everyone to pollute.' Implicit in this message is the notion that some are entitled (and have been entitled) to pollute more than others, all in the cause of development, economic growth, and material accumulation. Not only do rich countries extract a disproportionately large share of natural resources (water, wood, coal, land, minerals, etc.) but they also contribute a disproportionately large share to global pollution levels. The imbalanced nature of worldwide pollution shares is particularly evident in current levels of carbon dioxide (CO_2) and other greenhouse gas emissions.

Despite the fact that rich countries are the major emitters of greenhouse gases, increasing emission levels in less-wealthy countries, especially in the BRICs (Brazil, Russia, India, and China), are now of particular concern—to the countries of the global North. Most of the BRICs have registered an increase in greenhouse gases that by far exceed emission growth rates in developed countries. China, for example, has surpassed total CO_2 levels of the US and is now the top emitter in the world.

Once heavy industry, manufacturing, and petrochemical production were outsourced to the distant South, developed

—

countries were able to curtail emissions on a national scale. Of course, the problem has just been relocated geographically— to countries that now receive the blame for environmental degradation and atmospheric pollution. Moving factories to the South may look good in national environmental accounts of developed countries, but does not genuinely contribute to the tackling of climate change on a global scale.

In fact, emerging economies have become the 'pollution heavens' for most of the developed world's CO_2 emissions. China's export rates are well documented and we know that a significant amount of the country's carbon emissions are attributable to its immense export of manufactured products. The CO_2 emissions associated with the production of millions of plastic gadgets that are sitting in the global supermarket are attributed in international statistics to the country of production: China. About one third of China's CO_2 emissions are due to the production of export goods. Rich service economies of the North have conveniently outsourced both production and environmental costs to the South. Their remaining service sectors, however, remain intensely energy-hungry.

Outsourcing environmental costs to the South has also become common practice in the agriculture sector, which is one of the major drivers of methane (CH_4) emissions. While CO_2 is the primary anthropogenic greenhouse gas, CH_4 is widely acknowledged to have a global warming potential 21 times higher than CO_2 and is considered to be the largest potential contributor to global warming. The primary anthropogenic sources of CH_4 are agriculture (domestic livestock), landfill, and natural gas systems. New dietary patterns associated with high levels of meat consumption require a steady increase of livestock farming, which contributes significantly to an increase in CH_4 emissions. To satisfy the growing global demand for meat, fertile soils in the South have been transformed into grazing areas for livestock, leaving little land for growing edible food for the local communities.

Global activities in the agriculture sector are also a significant contributor to nitrous oxide (N_2O) emissions. According to

—

the Intergovernmental Panel on Climate Change (IPCC), soil management—in particular fertilizer use—contributes 69 per cent of human-induced N_2O emissions. A shift towards industrial agriculture in the South has led to increased fertilizer use and in turn to an unprecedented level of atmospheric N_2O concentration. Instead of spreading livestock manure on crop land, industrial farming relies heavily on climate-damaging fertilizers. Paradoxically, feed crops are grown in the South to feed livestock in the North. While livestock grows and manure accumulates (as waste) in the North, the South ends up with high concentrations of chemical fertilizers on crop-growing soils, degrading previously fertile land and setting free climate-damaging N_2O emissions.

The environmental and moral matter with outsourcing emissions to the global South are not just the immediate local impacts but also the distant effects of global warming to be expected. While the North has the technological and economic capacity to adapt to the adverse effects of climate change, the South will most likely suffer most from it. The vulnerability of poor countries is most obvious in their limited ability to react to extreme weather events. In Bangladesh, for example, the 2007 cyclone reportedly caused the death of 3,400 people and a cyclone of similar magnitude in 1991 cost the lives of another 140,000.

A changing climate also has significant effects on population health. Globally rising temperatures allow insects to move to higher altitudes, thereby bringing diseases such as malaria to previously unaffected regions and communities. The spread of meningitis, diarrhea, and dengue fever, and especially malaria, is in many cases associated with global warming, and estimated to increase significantly, particularly in poor countries. As sociologist Ulrich Beck pointed out in *The risk society*, the risk producers tend to suffer far less than the risk victims.

Given the disastrous effects of global warming, an immediate reduction (or at least stabilization) of greenhouse gas concentrations is inevitable if we are to prevent a global climatic and human tragedy. The most effective action would be to

—

reduce absolute levels of greenhouse gas emissions by simply burning less fossil fuel. But this is much easier said than done as there are two insurmountable obstacles: the existing levels of gross overconsumption in the North, and the promotion of resource-intensive consumption in the South. Under the current development ethos, it almost seems impossible to curtail global emissions while simultaneously boosting consumption in both the global North and South.

Feeling guilty for overconsumption?

Who takes the blame for wrecking the planet? An answer to this question has been offered by *Greendex*, an international survey among 17 developed and emerging economies to identify attitudes, consumption behaviors, and material lifestyles.

In terms of sustainable behaviour the index ranks US citizens last, Indian citizens first, and Chinese citizens second. The data suggest that sustainable consumption is more widely practised in emerging economies than in their economically higher developed counterparts. This is disenchanting news for ecological modernization theorists who stress that higher levels of economic development correspond to greater sustainability. Apparently, the opposite is the case: economic growth brings about lower levels of sustainable behaviour.

What is even more stunning is that the main polluters (people in rich countries) seem to experience less guilt for their consumption choices than their counterparts in poor countries. US citizens, for example, rank last in sustainable behaviour but are least likely to feel guilt for the implications of their consumption choices. This suggests that there are significant differences in how emerging markets and developed countries conceive environmental problems and responsibilities. One important task therefore is to first reconcile diverging experiences of environmental problems before any significant progress in environmental agreements can be made.

—

The unsustainability of 'sustainable development'

The examples highlighted above—ecological, food, and atmospheric scarcity—show that overconsumption has a number of detrimental social and environmental effects in both rich and poor countries, with the former generally responsible for creating the problems that the latter then have to deal with. Through deforestation, logging, biofuel production, meat consumption, pollution, and excessive extraction of natural resources, the global North has exploited the resources and absorptive capacity of the global South. Relentless overconsumption, the expansion of the market economy, and so-called 'environmentally friendly' growth policies imposed by the North have increasingly undermined self-sufficiency and ecological balance in the South.

Many argue that the time has come to rethink the idea of Northern 'giving' and to replace it with the idea of Northern 'restriction.' As Jean Ziegler has put it: "It is not a matter of giving more to the people in the South, but of taking less from them." Following this argument, the key to global sustainability is for the North to consume less, not for the South to consume more. But to bypass restriction, we build on something else: efficiency, and preferably, 'green efficiency.'

The push for **green efficiency** sounds intriguing, but on closer inspection it turns out to be fundamentally flawed. First, producing the same amounts of goods more efficiently does not contribute to the ultimate goal of humanity: genuine wellbeing. The rise of the global consumer culture has resulted in an explosion of goods but has failed to substantially increase levels of wellbeing. Studies associated with the New Economy Foundation have shown that the marginal increase of happiness is only significant up to US$15,000 per capita and then ceases or even declines. Happiness, whatever it is, probably cannot be measured and associated with any fixed standard. But even this imperfect indicator confirms the common-sense intuition that money isn't everything. Second, the gains won by increased efficiency will hardly ever suffice to compensate for rising levels

—

of consumption. And yet mainstream development experts argue that (green) consumption will lift the whole world out of poverty.

In its most basic definition consumption is understood as the private purchase and use of goods and services. A more holistic conception of consumption, however, goes beyond the mere act of purchase and usage, and begins with the emergence of consumer needs, desires, and wants and ends at the final disposal of goods. In this *needs–disposal continuum* lies an array of consumer activities; in the words of Wolfgang Sachs, all consumer goods have to be "chosen, bought, set up, used, experienced, maintained, tidied away, dusted, repaired, stored, and disposed of."

By introducing institutions of consumption, many traditionally living and communal-oriented societies are being transformed into consumerist societies based on Northern archetypes. This brings a whole new array of individualizing traits with it and delineates communities from their traditional lives. This model of development captures indigenous communities and converts them into what historian Peter Stearns calls "consumerist societies," in which "many people formulate their goals in life partly through acquiring goods that they clearly do not need for subsistence or for traditional display. They become enmeshed in the process of acquisition shopping—and take some of their identity from a procession of new items that they buy and exhibit," as he wrote in his 2001 *Consumerism in world history*.

At first glance, it seems that more recent developments, such as the emergence of sustainable consumption, are genuine attempts to transform consumerist cultures into more sustainable and self-reflective societies. At the 1992 Earth Summit in Rio almost all countries of the world embraced the idea of *sustainable development* and declared their genuine support. More than 20 years later, the catchword 'sustainable development' is still broadly understood as being synonymous with sustained economic growth. As the economist David Pearce, author of the British government's *Blueprint for a green economy*, put it: "sustainable development ... [is] fairly simply defined. It is continuously rising, or at least non-declining, consumption per capita, or GDP, or whatever the agreed indicator of development is." He

—

concludes that "... this is how sustainable development has come to be interpreted by most economists addressing the issue."

The ideology behind 'sustainable solutions' is embedded in most of the mainstream proposals: increase efficiency, promote recycling, tax polluters, offer incentives for adaptation, raise awareness, promote environmentally friendly goods ... in short, **Copenhagenize** the world. What fits less conveniently is anything that undermines economic growth: sufficiency, de-commodification of goods and services, voluntary restraint, capability approaches or de-growth. But there is little room in today's development discourse for what are perceived as utopian and Pollyannaish ideas. Alternative models are regarded as threats to the current economic configuration and considered archenemies of economic growth.

Some identify the conflict between capital and nature as the major cause of the present ecological crisis. Ecofeminist Giovanna Ricoveri, for example, suggests that "people are also part of nature, and the exploitation of nature is therefore also exploitation of some people by other people. Ecological degradation is also the degradation of human relationships." If this is true, the hypothesized relationship between ecological and human degradation bears a disenchanting consequence: as long as development is defined in terms of economic growth, which in turn is based on resource exploitation, development can by definition never advance to a genuine, humane enterprise.

As long as development builds on ecological exploitation it will always result in the degradation of people, no matter if this is done in a green way or not. If the very foundations of development rest on the dissemination of economic growth, rising food prices, and increasing resource scarcity are likely to continue.

Putting an end to scarcity

Poverty alleviation through consumption and (green) efficiency is a flawed approach. Strategies of this type are invariably self-defeating, eventuating in the opposite of what is desired: competition over scarce resources, inequality, and atmospheric pollution. What is much needed instead are new ways of social organization and more sensitive patterns of resource use—comprising principles of sufficiency, de-materialization, and indigenous modes of social organization. Most of these principles are embedded in the cultural narrative that is commonly known as *postdevelopment*. Conscious about the limits to growth (as a measure of development), many postdevelopment theorists are highly critical about the necessity of growth.

Social growth criticism challenges the assumption that economic growth and social wellbeing are inevitably related. The key argument is that above a certain level of consumption, the negative social and ecological effects of consumption offset the benefits. By challenging the relationship between economic growth and quality of life, social growth critics stress the importance of looking for models that decouple growth from wellbeing.

Ecological growth criticism points out the limits of the Earth's biocapacity and stresses that infinite growth (depending on natural resources exploitation) is simply impossible on a finite planet. The key argument is that consumption patterns that ignore the Earth's capacity to absorb waste and emissions will eventually ruin the ecological resources on which present and future generations depend.

The most radical proposal of a resource-light post-growth society is Serge Latouche's idea of ***décroissance***, which stimulated a lively political debate in France. In his recent book *Le temps de la décroissance* Latouche lays out the characteristics of a society that can do without growth and lives within its ecological means. He formulated eight principles that he sees as essential for a Habermasian decolonization of the lifeworld: re-evaluate, reconceptualize, restructure, redistribute, relocalize, reduce, reuse, recycle.

Political movements such as Objecteurs de Croissance and the French political party Décroissance have taken inspiration from de-growth models. Their political agendas comprise regionalization, de-globalization, de-commercialization, the regulation of capital markets, the abolition of the global financial

—

market, a reduction in resource use, the polluter pays principle, and internalization of ecological costs. Socioeconomic models adhering to post-growth ideologies put less pressure on the Earth's biocapacity and emphasize the local instead of the global. De-growth societies would help by freeing up resources and safeguarding traditional communities from being forced to adopt Northern modes of resource exploitation.

One major pillar of de-growth is sufficiency. Sufficiency strategies have recently entered mainstream debate as efficiency alone has proven insufficient to significantly advance human development. Sufficiency is commonly portrayed as completely contrary to efficiency. This dichotomization, however, is misleading as the two principles do not actually exclude each other. In fact, they could greatly complement each other. A combination of both strategies is perhaps the most promising way to curtail global throughput and unsustainable resource use.

Sufficiency is commonly understood as a lifestyle choice (for example, voluntary simplicity) and often grounded in the moralization of social and ecological issues. It means a retreat from consumption in absolute terms and a renouncement of many consumerist allurements. Proponents and practitioners aim to live up to values such as thrift, frugality, and self-reliance.

Sufficiency implies a focus on wellbeing rather than well-having. The frustration of well-having is, as Wolfgang Sachs has pointed out, that a simultaneous maximization of material and non-material satisfaction is virtually impossible. Every good purchased—no matter how small or big—requires a certain amount of time to be dealt with. Buying a new frying pan is one thing (material satisfaction), but finding the time to use the pan in preparing dinner for friends is another one (non-material satisfaction). Both material and non-material aspects of consumption require time. The problem is the widespread bias towards the material site (accumulating things) over the non-material site (experience and actual use).

While scarcity for many people in poor countries involves the struggle over food security and basic needs, many people in the rich countries of the global North are dealing with a shortage of a different type: time scarcity. In the North, the advent of a consumerist society has led to an abundance of material choices. This has been achieved at the expense of freedom of choice about time management. In the North, long working hours are not a means to cover basic needs, but to satisfy materialistic desires. Growth critics propose reducing working hours to 20 hours per week. It is speculated that if people are given the choice, many would decide against excessive income and goods. Instead they could enjoy more autonomy and arrange their daily lives in a more creative and self-fulfilling way. A reduction of working hours is seen as contributing to a less health-endangering life, more intense participation in political and social processes, an increase in voluntary work, more time for subsistence activities, a more equal distribution of work among men and women, and lower unemployment rates.

Apart from the opportunity for people to focus more on non-materialistic values, a reduction in working hours would also help to tackle ecological problems. Lower per capita incomes and a shift from a product to a service economy make people less reliant on natural resources extraction. The consumption-driven competition over resources would have a real chance to end.

The Lauderdale paradox

In his major work *An inquiry into the nature and origin of public wealth* (1804), James Maitland, 8th Earl of Lauderdale (1759-1839) argued that scarcity was necessary for a commodity to attain exchange value on the market. In his theory he distinguished between *public wealth* and *private riches* whereby the former consisted of "all that man desires that is useful or delightful to him" and the latter included "all that man desires that is useful or delightful to him, which exists in a degree of scarcity." For a commodity being classified as public wealth, it is sufficient to have a certain use value. Private riches, in contrast, require an exchange value as well.

The Lauderdale paradox argues that public wealth is inversely related to private riches. The assumption behind this argument is that the maximization of private riches works against the maximization of public wealth and welfare. A classic example presented by Lauderdale was the commodification of water. When water that was previously freely available was claimed by a man, it ceased to be a public good. Through its monopolization water acquired an exchange value associated with an increase in absolute scarcity of a formerly freely available good.

The Lauderdale paradox argues that independent of an increase of private riches the result would be a total loss of wealth for society as a whole. Attaching exchange values on freely available goods (for example, natural resources) would enhance private riches, but only at the expense of the common wealth. Applying this logic to the Earth's natural capital, all natural resources that become private riches would cease to be freely available—in order to obtain the same benefits from formerly freely available resources, one has now to purchase these benefits from private markets.

Taking less rather than giving more

If widely accepted figures are correct, more than 80 per cent of the planet's resources are consumed by less than 20 per cent of the world's population. These 80 per cent include resources coming from all around the world, not just those parts occupied by the 20 per cent. Raw materials, pre-manufactured goods, ready-made goods, and large amounts of foodstuff travel long distances to their final destinations of consumption in the North, and the remains usually travel back to the South for disposal. This odd pattern was created and sustained by trade liberalization, advances in technology, and free market globalization. Apart from the environmental and social costs of outsourcing extraction and disposal to the poorest, the associated transportation and logistics activities exacerbate global warming.

Under the present economic model, it appears illusive to replace this pattern with something healthier. It is obvious that the current culture of well-having is morally and environmentally alarming, and that a social model of wellbeing in which self-actualization is no longer exclusively attained through material accumulation is long overdue. We need to put models in place that can do without wrecking the bases for the lives of others only to sustain the reckless lifestyles of consumerist cultures. At the end of the day we cannot but deny the fact that resource scarcity is not an ecological, biological, chemical, or geological problem. It is an anthropogenic construction.

If rich people in the global North want to help poor people in the global South, they can best do so by taking less rather than by giving more. It makes no sense to destroy people's livelihoods, only to return like Santa Claus with a bag full of high-protein ready-to-eat meals. The people of the global North can promote both their own wellbeing and the wellbeing of others by consuming less and experiencing more.

Recommended reading

Done, A. (2012) *Global trends: Facing up to a changing world*, New York: Palgrave Macmillan.

Jackson, T. (2011) *Prosperity without growth: Economics for a finite planet*, London: Earthscan.

Jorgenson, A.K. and Clark, B. (2012) 'Are the economy and the environment decoupling? A comparative international study, 1960-2005,' *American Journal of Sociology*, vol 118, no 1, pp 1-44.

Latouche, S. (2010) 'Degrowth,' *Journal of Cleaner Production*, vol 18, no 6, pp 519-22.

Malthus, T.R. (1826) *An essay on the principle of population; Or, a view of its past and present effects on human happiness; with an inquiry into our prospects respecting the future removal or mitigation of the evils which it occasions* (6th edn), London: John Murray.

Meadows, D.H., Randers, J. and Meadows, D. (2004) *Limits to growth: The 30-year update*, White River Junction, VT: Chelsea Green.

Princen, T. (2005) *The logic of sufficiency*, Cambridge, MA: The MIT Press.

Sachs, W. (ed) (1993) *Global ecology—A new arena of political conflict*, London: Zed Books.

—

Sachs, W., Loske, R. and Linz, M. (1998) *Greening the north: A post-industrial blueprint for ecology and equity*, London: Zed Books.

Seidl, I. and Zahrnt, A. (eds) (2010) *Postwachstumsgesellschaft— Konzepte für die Zukunft*, Marburg: Metropolis.

Ziegler, J. (2003) *Die neuen Herrscher der Welt: und ihre globalen Widersacher*, Munich: C. Bertelsmann Verlag.

Ziegler, J. (2005) *Das Imperium der Schande: Der Kampf gegen Armut und Unterdrückung*, Munich: C. Bertelsmann Verlag.

FIVE

Reorganizing society from the bottom up

The enclosure of the commons in Britain, which marks the beginning of capitalism, evolved as a systematic effort to construct the individual as the basic unit of society and to organize society on the myth of the self-regulated market. This orientation produced the 19th-century experiment of unregulated, individualistic economics. The rise in trade globalization that followed at the end of the 19th and beginning of the 20th century had immense, overlapping consequences: the First World War, the Great Depression, and the Second World War. In order to close that cycle and to prevent more destruction, a new social pact was in order. For Karl Polanyi and other theorists the new pact would mean a profound transformation to a social economy, in which the risks of both Nazism and Stalinism were avoided. The pact took the form of Franklin Delano Roosevelt's New Deal, adopted in many countries in different forms and intensities.

The new arrangement assumed that some kind of economic coordination was indispensable. Three different agreements gave it its substance: the institutional integration of the working class, which implied both the official recognition of the unions and granting them an important voice in public policies; the principle of increased wages exchanged for increases in productivity; and the creation of the welfare state, investing in education, health, and other social services. The US was viscerally divided by debates on the New Deal, particularly about the new role of the workers and the government. But the arrangement produced what French analysts call "the 30 glorious years," an era of economic expansion with clear benefits for both capital and the workers in the three decades following the end of the Second World War.

The period between 1960 and 1973 can be seen as the golden years even among these glorious years, as the culmination of the unprecedented prosperity of the postwar period. It was a time in which everything was questioned: family, work, education, success, sanity, childcare, love, urbanism, science, technology, progress, and wealth. The new generation wanted to change everything. Dreams about the organic community, the adventure of ethnical diversity, respect for animal welfare and the environment, and modern technologies to reduce toil were dreamt about and brought to realization. In these years, the most dramatic, fast, and profound revolution of human affairs started and was partially realized; for most of humanity, it was as if the Middle Ages had suddenly come to an end. In this context, worker movements attempted to 'storm the heavens' and transcend the New Deal. They challenged the international division of labor with its unequal exchanges and its legacy of racism and sexism. They wanted a brand new world, beyond both capitalism and socialism.

And yet ... US corporations and wealthy individuals promoted everywhere the free market views of Polanyi's fellow Austro-Hungarian Friedrich Hayek (General Motors even produced a comic book version of his anti-planning manifesto, *The road to serfdom*) and made a god of the novelist-as-philosopher Ayn Rand. Since the Second World War they have created and funded a massive array of think tanks, business schools, and even entire universities to extol the virtues of the free market. A series of actions and bold policies, such as the dollar revaluation of Federal Reserve chairman Paul Volcker at the end of the 1970s, defeated the workers. Neoliberalism began. In just a few years all the arrangements of the New Deal were dismantled. Trade unions largely disappeared from the US economy and began to lose everywhere their role in public policies. Salaries and employment were first stagnant and then started to contract. Step-by-step the welfare society began to be dismantled. Former Conservative Prime Minister Margaret Thatcher boldly proclaimed that 'there is no such thing as society ... and people must look to themselves first.' And people did.

Just as Polanyi perceived the transformation to a social economy as a necessary reaction to the excesses of 19th-century free markets, social movements today, from Via Campesina to Occupy Wall Street, are reacting to the excesses of 21st-century neoliberalism. Polanyi, in *The great transformation*, called this the **double movement**:"the extension of the market organization in respect to genuine commodities [is] accompanied by its restriction in respect to fictitious ones," the fictitious being land, labor, and money. As grains, motorcycles, and hardware become commodities to be bought and sold on markets, people and communities seek to pull their homes, their leisure, and most of all, their labor out of the market sphere.

At the top, in the governments and the international institutions, the neoliberal discourse persists, but with a radical twist. As President Obama expressed in his first inauguration speech, the government is the only entity that can deal with the current problem. The market should be controlled and protected from its own excesses. A peculiar kind of statist neoliberalism concentrates the power and the resources of the governments in rescue operations of corporations 'too big to fail,' and in supporting their new incursions in 'virgin territories' where they can organize what social geographer David Harvey calls "accumulation by dispossession."

Mining as "accumulation by dispossession"

Mining is a classic example of this "accumulation by dispossession." In David Harvey's view, the rise of neoliberalism has made possible a "new imperialism" leading to the enrichment of a minority by depriving the majority of their wealth (for example, communal or indigenous land). Across the globe, mining companies take advantage of privatization, state redistribution, and neoliberal policies to develop and exploit mineral resources in areas that for centuries have been the homes of indigenous peoples and their cultures.

—

In many resource-rich regions, governments open their doors to foreign mining corporations in the hope of boosting their national economies. They seek to create a favourable environment for resource exploitation by transnational companies through the liberalization of mining laws and approvals of international trade treaties such as the **North American Free Trade Agreement** (NAFTA). By doing so, they hope to attract foreign investors promising job creation and infrastructure improvements. But corporations almost never deliver on those alluring promises.

Instead of jobs and wealth, mega-mining projects bring severe environmental and social costs to local communities. Most large-scale mining activities today are open-pit, which means wholesale deforestation through the clear cutting of forests and communal lands. Mining also involves using and disposing of huge amounts of water, associated with the contamination of soil, rivers, and aquifers with cyanide, arsenic, lead, or acid drainage. Further, extractive industry activities are commonly accompanied by immense social costs such as the displacement and relocation of communities. Uprooting communities from their territories wipes out cultures that are found in institutions, knowledge, and land ascribed with century-old cultural meaning.

To date, these adverse effects do not prevent governments drawing foreign investors from overseas to explore and exploit their mineral-rich lands. One of the greatest sell-outs of land is currently happening in Mexico, where some of the world's largest reserves of key minerals can be found. Mexico is one of the most popular exploration destinations and attracts significant foreign investment, in particular from Canadian mining giants, who make up 75 per cent of all foreign investment in the sector (according to a 2012 report from consulting firm Deloitte on the mining industry in Mexico). Mexico's recent liberalization of mining laws has prioritized foreign-owned resource extraction over the protected lands of communities to which it originally belongs. Through dubious methods and misleading local people about the consequences of exploitation projects, international mining corporations are given mining concessions of up to 50 years, with 100 per cent ownership of the capital stock.

—

Concession holders are officially entitled to clean land that is occupied by local communities, land that has for centuries been used for cultivation, rituals, and sacred purposes. This land can then legally be levelled. The absence of fair consultation of local communities on mining projects, the violation of international laws and treaties and the silencing of anti-mining movements through violent repression and the criminalization of public protests results in an atmosphere of violence. Recently, anti-mining movements have begun to organize globally and to redesign their resistance, arguing for a reinforcement of disrupted community structures such as assemblies, territorial control, and community authorities. Through the strengthening of these institutions, anti-mining movements hope to turn a development model dependent on extractive industries into a thing of the past. "Yes to life, no to mining," proclaimed hundreds of people from a dozen countries, on 13 January 2013, in the Encuentro de Pueblos de Mesoamérica, "Sí a la Vida, No a la Minería," held in Calpulalpan, Oaxaca in Mexico.

At the grassroots, everywhere, particularly throughout the poor countries of what the *New Internationalist* magazine likes to call the **majority world**, something like Polanyi's *double movement* is happening, but it only comes to the world's attention when something dramatic occurs—the shooting of 34 striking miners in South Africa, the refusal of farmers to make way for a car manufacturing plant in India, the rebellion of entire communities over environmental devastation in China—but it is bubbling along beneath the global media horizon all the time. In terms of sheer numbers, far more people are involved in anti-systemic movements than in propping up the market system itself.

Victory is never certain. Polanyi and most of his contemporaries were convinced that the free market had died with the 19th century, yet a century later market solutions once again dominate development discourses. Today communitarian social movements, many inspired by indigenous nations, are leading the effort to affirm the primacy of community over the individual as the unit of human welfare, opposing at the same time the collectivism that plagued the socialist experiment. Wherever these local struggles lead, there is increasing awareness about the need for a concerted action to

—

deal with the environmental and social crisis that overrides the individual's right to consume and the market's right to produce. The battle has not been won, but it is being fought, not by a single global community but by a global collection of communities and movements. Today's double movement against global capitalism is an amalgamation of local movements. Local societies are restricting the sphere of the global market—and successfully.

Insurrection against the market

A wide variety of initiatives are being experienced now, by people at the grassroots, all over the world. Well rooted in tradition and local culture, the social majorities are apparently departing from contemporary thinking and behavior. They are not attempting to come back to any lost paradise, nor are they falling into nostalgia or revivalism. They are dissolving the historical break—the rupture with the past—imposed by modernity. This search for continuity gives them the spirit of the old wine. But they are not merely new bottles. They come from different grapes and the wine is different. They are so new, in fact, that we have no words to express their initiatives in an articulate manner. Our formal categories are irrelevant or useless. Even our words, the doors of our perception, are not accurate. And that is our predicament.

In a sense, what we need to do is impossible. These experiences are so well rooted in local spaces and cultures that any attempt to reduce them to a single, global discourse is both impossible and preposterous. But they have in common something that goes beyond both modernity and postmodernity. What is happening defines a general reaction against a pathological social condition that has reached a world scale and is increasingly unbearable.

After modernity we may have the flourishing of a thousand different lifestyles, redefining what living well is in local, rooted terms. Hopefully, we will not have a universal, unique truth, nor global certainties of the kind now promoted by the global discourse of development; a thousand different truths, different perceptions of the world, different cosmic visions conceived at the local level, will emerge from the ruins left by modernity. But the differentiated responses we are now observing are reactions to a common enemy. Each of those diverse, dispersed struggles is focused against a different head of the modern Hydra.

An insurrection could thus be taking place, entirely evident but at the same time invisible. It could be underway right in front of our eyes, but we would not see it because of its novelty and the blinders and optical filters imposed by modernity. Polanyi's double movement against 19th-century liberalism was visible in the news because it was a reorganization of society from the top down. Today's double movement against 21st-century neoliberalism, by contrast, is a reorganization of society from the bottom up.

The common denominator connecting the current initiatives taking place at the grassroots around the world today can be thought of as the recovery of verbs. People are substituting verbs such as learning and healing for nouns such as education and health. The latter define 'needs' whose satisfaction depends on public or private entities that are increasingly incapable of satisfying them. The former express the recovery of personal and collective agency towards autonomous paths of social transformation.

From food consumption to 'eating'

We have reached a point, notes Uruguayan Eduardo Galeano, where those who do not fear hunger instead have a fear of eating: they are increasingly aware of what the market put on their plates, from horsemeat to 'pink slime,' and they are alarmed. People are reacting, and not just in the premium farmers' markets of London and New York. They know very well that the Monsantos and Walmarts of the world will not experience moral epiphanies and that governments will be unable to reform agribusiness—and even less to control or substitute for it.

Cultivating food in the cities is a very old tradition that is making a spectacular comeback. Hundreds of community gardens are prospering in Detroit, a city that clearly illustrates the limits of industrial development. In Thailand the Bangkok city government is teaching people to grow vegetables in plastic buckets. On a much larger scale, in the 1990s Cuban citizens discovered that after 30 years of modernist revolution they imported the majority of their food supply in addition to all of the required chemicals to support their highly industrialized agriculture. With the disappearance of Soviet imports, ordinary Cubans lost 5.5 kilos (according to a 2013 study in the *British Medical Journal*) or up to 10 kilos (according to anecdotal reports); whatever the truth of this figure there certainly was hunger, again, as before their socialist revolution. Today, by necessity if not by design, Cuban citizens have become the world champions of organic agriculture, with its cities producing more than half of what the urban inhabitants consume.

At the same time, people are creating alternatives to the food market by forming new connections between the countryside and the cities. Urban consumers are associating themselves with local producers. The contemporary design of these new units was apparently born in Germany and Japan, but has spread like an epidemic across the US (under the name 'community-supported agriculture') and Canada ('community-shared agriculture'). Tens of thousands of such groups already exist and are complemented by independent organic producers selling directly in nearby cities. This relationship, conceived as a way to lose our fear of eating, has acquired such a dynamic that even Walmart is attempting to mimic and control it.

In the countryside of Africa, Asia, and Latin America the struggle for land is spreading and intensifying. At times it has taken the form of a silent occupation, more or less clandestine, such as the one that recently took place in Peru: indigenous peoples recovered 1 million hectares and are currently producing 40 per cent of the country's food supply using traditional practices. In other cases spectacular struggles with uncertain results have taken place, as in the struggles of Chinese farmers against urbanization, desertification, pollution, land seizures, and the diversion of water for industrial uses. Meanwhile all around the Indian Ocean basin, from Madagascar to India to Indonesia, indigenous farmers have been mobilizing to protect their lands (and their production methods) from forced conversion to corporate industrial agriculture.

More and more communities are now resisting the expropriation of their lands and their ways of life by the global neoliberal elite. As they do so, they are reaffirming the value of their community assemblies, the principle of public office as community service, the communal ownership of land and a reconstitution of peoples' territories. The Quito Declaration, formulated in October 2009 by the International Commission of Integral Agrarian Reform, illustrates the attitudes that blame the chemical-intensive Green Revolution and subsequent commercialization policies for the food crises the world has experienced in recent years. The people are denouncing the contamination and privatization of water by large corporations while affirming the farmers' struggles for agrarian reform and the defence of their territories.

Via Campesina, the largest organization of farmers in history, frames the issue of eating within the notion of food sovereignty. It is expressed in rather simple terms: we should define for ourselves what we eat, and produce it on our own terms. The same path has been taken by the World Organization of Fishermen, again the largest of its kind in history. Given the current condition of the world, in which a large portion of the population has surrendered itself to diets and eating practices that are imposed by capital and its production systems, few proposals are as radical and complex as that of food sovereignty. By actively eating, rather than passively consuming, food, we transform the traditional quest for self-sufficiency and give it a more radical and political content. Hunger for some and obesity and diabetes for others are conflated in the same struggle. As Eduardo Galeano has observed, no one will die of hunger because no one will die of indigestion.

From education to 'learning'

Education systems everywhere are in crisis; they marginalize a majority of the people and do not adequately prepare them for work or for life. This is as true of schools in rich countries as it is of schools in poor ones. School systems mostly produce dropouts; more than half of the children who currently enrol do not attain the minimum educational levels considered acceptable for full participation in society in their respective countries. This enforces a permanent discrimination against large segments of the population because they lack the passport provided by an appropriate degree, which is essential for navigating modern society.

Those who learn to consume the commodity called 'education' can accumulate up to 20 years of 'seat-time' for a diploma but still not find work. Those who do find work rarely work in their areas of education. Nonetheless, despite this obvious failure of the world's schools and the damage it provokes, a general struggle for 'educational access' persists. The majority has been educated into the idea that this is the only way they can succeed in society. So Pakistani parents continue to clamour for meaningless pidgin English classes for their children, confident that English is their passport to higher incomes and better lives; Chinese students who will never be mathematicians or concert pianists cram for mathematics exams and piano recitals; Americans of all classes are subjected to endless rounds of standardized tests.

Global campaigns to convince parents to send their children to school have been, and continue to be, successful in all except the most war-torn and socially disorganized countries. But the schools themselves cannot satisfy the demand so created. Even in rich countries such as the UK the government refuses to devote the resources necessary to meet the educational aspirations of poor students and their parents. In most poor countries, neither the facilities nor the human resources exist to properly educate all the children who want to be educated, even if the will were to be found. In Maharashtra in India even such a well-resourced overseas organization such as the British Council has reportedly been unable to recruit a sufficient number of teachers to staff its language education initiatives.

People are reacting. Students, parents, and teachers are attempting to reform and broaden the dominant educational system, to change its theories and practices, both public and private, from within. They challenge teachers' unions, administrators, corporations, and the state—all of which seek to transform education systems to serve their own interests. Other groups struggle inside and outside of the state and market in order to drive forth different forms of 'alternative education.'

Meanwhile a vigorous, growing movement is advancing in another direction. The practices of autonomous and liberated learning have become more popular than ever. The movement is generating its own institutional arrangements at the margins, against, and beyond the system. Supported by their own theoretical apparatuses, such practices go well beyond existing frameworks, reclaiming ancient learning traditions and integrating contemporary technologies in promoting ways to learn and study as free and joyful activities.

This is indeed a unique movement. It is possibly the biggest on earth, in terms of the number of people involved. But it is basically invisible, and a large part of those participating in it do not feel like they are part of local social or political movements, much less a global one, even though they love to find others like themselves, engage in horizontal relationships and share experiences with them. The movement itself is generating new centers for the production of knowledge outside public and private research centers and conventional institutions. They are developing new technologies based on significant theoretical innovations that reformulate the world's perception and introduce new methodologies to interact with it that challenge dominant paradigms.

As Foucault suggested, this is an expression of the insurrection of subordinated knowledge, which strengthens and deepens it. Parents and children are reclaiming the historical content buried or masked within functional coherences and formal systematizations. They are revaluing knowledge that had been disqualified from formal curricula because it had been considered useless, insufficiently elaborated, naive, or hierarchically inferior to scientific knowledge. They are juxtaposing and combining learned knowledge with local memory, erudite with empirical knowledge, to form an historical knowledge of struggle.

This requires the demolition of the tyranny of globalising discourses with its hierarchy and privileges derived from the scientific classification of knowledge. Education will still go on in schools, but increasingly, learning is moving outside them. Whether it is through the intergenerational transmission of indigenous knowledge, a teach-in held at an Occupy protest, self-study using Wikipedia, or simply one neighbour talking to another, real learning is moving out of the classroom and back into society. As formal education becomes ever more poorly resourced, as schools and universities are increasingly turned over to corporations to be run for profit, as the provision of education by the state falls further and further behind the aspirations of the population, learning is inevitably replacing education as the key to personal intellectual fulfilment.

From healthcare to 'healing'

Healthcare systems around the world are increasingly inefficient, discriminatory, and counterproductive. The iatrogenic effect is increasingly documented: doctors and hospitals (and the system in which they are embedded) are producing more diseases than they cure. What caused great scandal when Ivan Illich published *Medical nemesis* 40 years ago has now become a common personal experience. Most lung cancer is caused not by inscrutable genetic mutations, but by the industrial scale production and promotion of cigarettes. Type II diabetes is not caused by insulin resistance, or even by overeating; it is caused by the commodification of food and the forced sedentary lifestyles of modern society. The healthcare industry has a vested interest in creating and maintaining disease so that it can manage and 'cure' it. Manageable but incurable diseases are the most profitable of all.

The production, distribution, and consumption of healthcare is one of the largest economic sectors in most of the countries of the world, and involves a growing number of people. The medical profession and the healthcare industry have taken control of every institutional apparatus: they formulate the norms of appropriate behaviour in life and in death, apply them in total institutions from which most people have little hope of escape, and punish those who violate them with withdrawal of treatment—or worse. Each failure of this professional dictatorship offers the opportunity to strengthen and spread it further. And the failures multiply every day.

People's efforts to resist the industrialization of healthcare have taken many different avenues. As in the case of education, innumerable efforts are underway to reform the system from the inside, many of them frustratingly ineffective. Passionately dedicated nurses, doctors, and public health professionals throughout the world promote preventative medicine and 'cures' as simple as eating well and regular walking, but there is usually no money to be made in prevention. Similarly, there has been a proliferation of alternative therapies that try to avoid the dominant system's most damaging (and most costly) effects. In most cases, however, the results are counterproductive, deepening the pathogenic character of the search for health.

In countries that lack functioning mass healthcare systems—that is to say, in the vast majority of the countries of the world—traditional therapies that have been marginalized and disqualified by the health professions are now being recovered. These often enable healthier behaviour patterns and more humane forms of treatment that are rooted in the home and community. These efforts are already shaping institutional arrangements, for example, in sub-Saharan Africa, where formal health services do not reach the majority of the population. Instead, most people rely on traditional healers, who may not be able to cure diseases such as AIDS or malaria but who can help reduce symptoms such as fever, providing palliative care.

In both of the world's two most populous countries, India and China, the majority of the population relies on traditional practices, not Western medicine. This is neither a value nor a scientific judgement (although it may be both); it is a fact of life. Meditation, massage therapy, aromatherapy, and acupuncture are first-line treatments, not alternative therapies. They have their own academies, professional associations, and established practices. They are where people go for healing, if not necessarily for healthcare as such. In fact, some studies show that the number one malady that leads Africans to consult traditional healers is plain 'bad luck.'

At issue is not whether the care available from traditional healers in villages that are many hours' walk from the nearest bush clinic is as effective as the care available to those who can afford to pay for it at the Mayo Clinic or the Johns Hopkins Hospital. At issue is whether the care available from traditional healers is as effective as the care available from local allopathic providers who have been partially educated in Western medical practice and who may or may not have access to genuine (non-counterfeit) drugs. A further issue is the (un-)affordability of Western medicine and drugs. The best advice for people living in poor countries is probably not to get sick in the first place.

And not getting sick is increasingly what they are trying to do. China and India have seen the emergence of organized environmental activism on a scale unimaginable in the global North. People aren't just 'liking' their favourite causes on Facebook. They are protesting, blockading, and dying to prevent the expansion of polluting industries. In Indonesia, indigenous resistance against the expansion of coalmines and palm oil plantations is largely focused on the preservation of population health. In Mexico the Lacandón Mayan nation has sought to preserve the Montes Azules Biosphere Reserve as a way of preserving their healthy traditional diet. Rebelling against the neoliberal model of health as a commodity to be purchased, people around the world are seeking to heal themselves of wounds that have often been inflicted in the name of development.

From housing development to 'settling'

The disasters associated with public and private development projects are proliferating around the world, increasing the number of homeless people everywhere, from London and New York to Cape Town and São Paulo. In the rich cities of the global North the juxtaposition of homelessness with overbuilding has given rise to squatters' movements—otherwise homeless people settling in unwanted so-called 'brownfield' sites that are awaiting further development. In the poorer cities of the global South homelessness has resulted in the mass building of shantytowns— otherwise homeless people settling in unwanted literally brown field sites adjacent to the developed properties of the rich. In both rich and poor countries, the homeless are settling—whether the state wants them to or not.

In South Africa the withdrawal of the Landless People's Movement from the state has been formalized in the "No Land! No House! No Vote!" campaign. Faced with a government that does not provide basic public services, the participants have withdrawn from national politics. They face teargassing, beatings, arrest, or imprisonment in order to affirm their right to settle. In Latin America the squatters' movement has been formalized under the banner *autoconstrucción* (building for oneself). Slum-dwellers in Kenya are highly organized and are demanding formal recognition of their rights to the properties in which they live. In India there is a movement towards tenure security that, while falling short of *de jure* legal title, is in practice a *de facto* recognition of people's rights to settle.

Nowhere has the self-organization of ordinary people for the right to settle occurred on so large a scale as in contemporary China. Settlers' movements in China are little reported in the rest of the world due to China's secure grip on all domestic media, combined with the fact that international NGOs simply cannot operate in China. Chinese people's assertion of their rights to settle and resistance to eviction for development has thus been a wholly indigenous affair that cannot be credited to kind-hearted Western supporters. A few high-profile evictions in the internationalized cities of Beijing and Shanghai have received Western press attention, but the demographic center of gravity of the settlement movement lies further to the east in the less-visited interior of China. Ordinary Chinese people are fighting one of the most brutally centralized developmentalist regimes in the world—and often winning. The Chinese government, always with an eye looking back to 1989, is quick to jail individual dissidents but reluctant to enforce its will against ordinary people organizing against eviction for development.

The most dramatic manifestation of ordinary people's determination to settle rather than wait for housing to be provided for them, however, is probably the pure grit shown by Haitians in the wake of the 2010 earthquake. In the immediate aftermath of the earthquake the world opened its heart to Haiti, with governments pledging US$4.5 billion in aid to rebuild the country. 'Our goal must be the empowerment of the Haitian people' declared US Secretary of State Hillary Clinton. Meanwhile her husband, former President Bill Clinton, was busy promoting foreign investment in extra-legal export processing zones. Two years on, less than half the promised reconstruction aid had actually been received.

Not content to wait for the hundreds of thousands of new, weatherproof homes promised by international donors, Haitians have quickly resettled, building homes using materials at hand, if necessary, salvaged timber and plastic tarps. These are not perfect homes. But they are better than the tents provided by disaster relief agencies, and better than the non-existing weatherproof homes their government promised to build with international funds. They are homes, however flimsy, and they allow families to settle down and to get on with family life. The main problem is that these new homes are often built on land that is technically owned by the country's oligarchical elite or slated by the government for foreign industrial development. Facing eviction, Haitians have organized to protect their rights to settle. Their homes may not be beautiful, but they are homes.

The ultimate insurrection against the market: 'exchanging'

Although the **Walmartization** of the world continues, a new era of direct exchange is spreading outside of the capitalist economy. Social markets where producers and consumers abandon their abstract conditions to engage in direct interaction with other people are proliferating. Some are even abandoning the direct use of money as commodity and replacing it with social exchanges of goods or labor between parties who know and trust one another. Such initiatives openly defy the fiction of the self-regulated market and attempt to escape completely from corporate domination. This kind of exchanging is far from dominant in people's economic lives, but that is beside the point. The point is that they are bringing the market inside the social sphere, socializing the market rather than marketizing the social. The more people come to think of the market as a socially embedded aspect of life, the less power the market has over society, and ultimately over life itself.

Beyond postmodernity

In exploring peace, Wolfgang Dietrich has been exploring for years the switch from postmodernity to postmodernism, that is, from the postmodern condition to the postmodern cognition. Postmodernism, for him, is not an epoch that follows modernity but an aspect of the modern condition itself.

"If modernity," he writes, "is understood as the societal project characterized by Newtonian physics, Cartesian reductionism and the nation state of Thomas Hobbes, then postmodernity does not stand for an epoch which is equipped with a new paradigm of comparable efficacy and a comparable claim to truth. Instead, postmodernity simply refers to that disillusioning phase of the same modernity in which people increasingly doubt the universal truth of this paradigm. These doubts, and this perception, derive mostly from everyday experience, that is, they stand for an important intellectual and social achievement, without being immediately the result of scholarly reflection in a more narrow, institutional sense."

Such disillusionment can be experienced as a loss of values and orientation, the anomie explored by classical sociologist Émile Durkheim. Despite the political, social, and psychological consequences of such anomie, social scientists refused to break with conventional truths and argued instead for higher doses of the same remedies, assuming that more development, progress, justice, democracy, technology, universal values, and capitalism were enough to reach paradise on earth. The 'end of history,' as suggested by Francis Fukuyama in the 1990s, implied that humanity could not get or even conceive anything better than the marriage of capitalism with liberal democracy.

While academia continues with the exploration, conceptualization, and interpretation of social reality, tending time and again to reduce it to the 'old truths' of modernity, people by the millions are creating new social realities with corresponding social paradigms, leaving behind the social paradigm within which they were colonized, enclosed, exploited, marginalized, and oppressed. They are beginning to enclose the enclosers. In a very real sense, they are already beyond both modernity and postmodernity.

Recovering a sense of proportion

Leopold Kohr, founder of the theory of social morphology, said long ago that economic fluctuations are not due to classic business cycles but to the actual scale of the economic activity. Rather than simple economic cycles, we now have size crises. Economic integration and the growth and expansionary effect of government controls do not reduce or shorten these cycles; on the contrary, they magnify them. Whether or not this is 'scientifically' true, the irresponsible arrogance and greed of the past 30 years have brought the world to a dead end. The government controls currently applied to correct market behaviours could only be successful if there was a clear vision of what is to be controlled within appropriate safety margins, and these conditions are no longer possible.

If the problems currently faced by the world economy are a matter of sheer size and unregulability, what needs to be done is to reduce the size of the political and economic bodies that generates such devastating scale. The world needs preventative action to reduce the size of potential economic problems more than it needs additional regulation to handle them after the fact. The idea is to make the scale of industry proportionate to the limited human ability for managing it. Neither the President of the US nor the President of the Deutsche Bank is likely to be able to name all of the countries in which his organization operates, never mind understand those operations in detail.

Scale and proportion are also central in another aspect. Returning policy and ethics back to the center of social life can only be done in the midst of real, lived entities, such as the community. Attempting to do this at the scale of abstract entities, such as the multinational organization or the nation-state, is impossible and counter-productive. Ethics require norms, and norms can only be formed and enforced among people who are in regular contact with each other. Senators and chief executive officers can hardly be expected to have any visceral understanding of the poverty that exists in their midst, even among the many servants in their many homes and offices.

The case of peace and violence illustrates the nature of the problem. The *Pax Romana* signified a contract of domination: "I will not destroy you, as long as you accept my rules." The *Pax Americana*—to the extent that it is a peace at all—is based on the same principle. Among the countries of the global North this is the dominant notion of peace, as can be seen today in Honduras, Gaza, Iran, or wherever in Africa there is oil to be found.

If we recognize the plurality of the real world and the postmodern condition—beyond the universalist paradigm and the celebration of difference—we have to recognize the culturally rooted character of social functions that can be associated with what is called peace: there are peaces, not peace. At a national or international scale 'peace' is only a disguise for a permanent war, suspended. What we need to construct is an agreement for the harmonious coexistence of different cultures, each of which possesses its own notion of 'peace' and claims, above all, to be 'left in peace.' Such agreement corresponds to the worlds being created by indigenous nations, worlds in which many worlds can be embraced.

Indigenous nations have a built-in sense of proportion because the individuals who comprise an indigenous nation share an organic culture, a culture reproduced through living rather than a culture spread from above through formal education and commercial mass media. Indigenous nations have also had to learn to live as nations within larger, often hostile colonial states. For most indigenous nations, verbs such as eating, learning, healing, and settling are the recreation of culture, not of consumption. They have never accepted the primacy of the market, and thus don't need a second, double movement to react against it. Indigenous nations provide a ready-made model of **localization** with which to fight the universalism of the market. They are today a source of inspiration for all the non-indigenous people interested in forging the new condition.

Pondering the alternative path

The very Leninist conviction that the state is the main agent for social change and the main object of political activity is still popular. The state is often perceived as a simple structure of mediation: a means ready to dance the tune others play. It is fascist if controlled by the fascists, socialist in the hands of the socialists, and democratic if one believes it reflects one's own values. As the Greek communist Nicos Poulantzas had it, "let the people get rid of the usurpers and the state will take care of everything." Poulantzas meant this ironically, but too many people take it literally. The problem is not a small elite of corrupt oligarchs who use the state for their own ends. The problem is the state itself.

The nation-state, from the harshest dictatorships to the most genuine and pure democracies, has been and continues to be a structure of domination and control imposed on the people to put them in service of capital. It was designed for this purpose and absorbed and perverted all the diverse forms of state and nation created before. The state is the ideal collective capitalist, guardian of its interests. Even in the most modern democratic states it operates as a dictatorship, or at best as a benevolent dictatorship. How many of the 200-odd countries of the world can be said to have clean government, government of the people, by the people, for the people? Ten? Five? Any? From an empirical standpoint, what we call democracy would be better described as democratic despotism.

In the midst of the Second World War, German philosopher Walter Benjamin observed that the state of exception, the state of emergency in which the rights of minorities and the poor could be disregarded or trampled, was not the exception but the rule. More recently the Italian philosopher Giorgio Agamben has reminded us that the supposedly exceptional regime is now an ordinary characteristic of contemporary societies. New categories of people are continually identified and deprived of their rights; migrants, for example, continually fall into that condition. With drug trafficking or international terrorism as a pretext, the exclusion is applied to more and more categories of people. *Homo oeconomicus* has become *Homo sacer*, liable to be deprived of life or liberty at any moment.

The British writer John Berger wrote in a 2011 essay in *Guernica* magazine that if he was forced to use one word to describe the current condition of the world, he would feel the need to call it a prison.

It has been four decades since Foucault opened a line of reflection on power that we did not dare to follow, fully assuming the consequences of his reflection. He demonstrated, among other things, that instead of separating the legal from the illegal, the law does nothing but create forms of illegality as class privileges. We have been led to believe that laws are made to be respected and, furthermore, that the purpose of the police and courts is to make sure they are in fact respected. But whose laws?

It is not enough to know that the laws are made by some and imposed on the rest. We must discover, as well, the fallacy inherent in that sacrosanct term, 'rule of law.' The production of illegality, encompassing ever more areas of the public realm, is no imperfection or accident, but an integral part of the functioning of market society. All laws distinguish between the spaces where laws can be violated or ignored (by some) and those where offenses can be punished (for the rest). A minor bureaucrat's demand for payment to process a form is condemned as corruption. A national leader's sweetheart privatization of public assets to friends and relatives is applauded as market liberalization.

In one country after another, the increasingly cynical political classes adopt measures and enact laws to increase the privileges of those who can violate or ignore the law and widen the realm within which ordinary citizens are exposed to arbitrary power and incarceration. The social framework of civil and political rights constructed over centuries of struggle is being dismantled to promote 'the market.' The fourth world war anticipated by the Zapatistas has already arrived, but with no trumpets, no declarations, not even a press conference. It is a war in which the people themselves have been identified as the enemy, the market the protagonist.

The Anjuman-e-Mazareen-e-Punjab (Association of Punjab's Tenants), a peasant movement in Pakistan's Punjab region, is rooted in a very old tradition of peasant resistance that takes a contemporary form in the context of globalization. In reclaiming their land and a form of sovereignty, they share the universal disenchantment with formal democracy, the political parties and the government. They no longer deposit their hopes in the state apparatuses and are not interested in capturing them. In reclaiming control of their own lives, they look for a different form of self-organization and self-rule. This extends to the field of law and justice: they operate 'people's law tribunals' called *saths*. These were created when the people found it was useless to speak to power to ask it to address its own failures. As Law Professor Asad Farooq explains in a 2013 interview:

'We have this fetish that either the state is the institution that crafts and administers the law or that people are governed through customary law. These people's tribunals were outside these two categories. They were deeply imbricated in the political struggle, and the political struggle is what gave it its shape and its flavour. The beauty of these tribunals is that they reclaim the crafting of law, reclaim the ability to actually say "we are the ones who do law, we are the ones who want to articulate judgements and we are the ones who craft the law that stems from that.'"

Initiatives for resistance and liberation have been facing first and foremost the "intimate enemy" described by Ashis Nandy in his 1983 book of the same title, the internalized visions and perceptions with which we have been colonized. The struggle itself and the new world should not be conceived from the top down. We need to completely surrender ourselves to the creativity of real, ordinary people, who are, in the end, those who make revolutions and create the new worlds. What happens with the whole of society is always the result of innumerable initiatives and factors that are almost always unpredictable. Perhaps the most radical Zapatista affirmation is that which says that they are just common, everyday people, ordinary folks, and are, hence, non-conformist, rebels, dreamers. This affirmation shows us a clear alternative to the Leninist paradigm that dominated the world in the 20th century.

The ongoing insurrection does not call for sudden shifts in power or policies. It asks instead for a new attitude: reclaiming a sense of proportion and common sense—the sense you have in community. It implies, as James Scott would say, to stop seeing like a state, from the top down. It means to see the world from where we are, with feet on the ground, and acknowledging who we are: simple mortals.

As the late Howard Zinn reminded us, revolutionary change does not come as one cataclysmic moment, but as an endless succession of surprises, moving zigzag towards a more decent society.

The road to serfdom and *The great transformation*

The break-up of the Austro-Hungarian empire after the First World War bequeathed to Anglo-American thought two of the most influential writers on society of the 20th century. From the Austrian side came Friedrich Hayek, author of *The road to serfdom*. From the Hungarian side came Karl Polanyi, author of *The great transformation*. Both books were published in 1944, at a time when the ultimate Nazi defeat was viewed as all but certain, and both books were received as blueprints for the postwar order to come.

Both books harkened back to the 19th century, for Hayek a golden age of market capitalism and for Polanyi a dark age of social destruction. Hayek thought that social planning of all kinds deprived people of the freedom to make their own decisions in life and that labor unions were some of the worst institutions of all, since in his view, when workers banded together for mutual benefit, they implicitly deprived others by seizing more of society's surplus. In this, Hayek seemingly viewed the social economy in zero-sum games: what's good for me must be bad for you.

Polanyi, on the other hand, argued that if "industrialism is not to extinguish the race, it must be subordinated to the [social] requirements of man's nature." Polanyi viewed people in primarily optimistic terms: he thought that people needed (and wanted) more than just to pursue their personal self-interests. This impulse could be channelled into a striving for common good (such as socialism) or into a striving for the subordination of others (such as militarism) but either way, the impulse would get out. "The discovery of society is thus either the end or the rebirth of freedom."

Much of *The great transformation* focuses on the changes over time in England's anti-poverty provisions and how they helped define England's labor markets. Polanyi argued that the Speenhamland system of guaranteed living wages from 1795-1834 softened the impact of the Industrial Revolution by preventing the full commodification of labor. With the passage of the 1834 Poor Law Reform, the England we have come to know as 'Dickensian' came into existence: in place of a bread subsidy, the poor were given time in workhouses or prisons.

Polanyi considered mid-19th-century England to be the high point of free market capitalism. What he would have made of today's welfare-to-work programs we don't know, but we can certainly guess. He would have been horrified by US anti-poverty programs, which generally consist of a few years of forced minimum wage employment for women with young children and nothing at all for anyone else. For Polanyi, freedom meant the freedom to take a job or leave it, and people only have that freedom if they won't starve without a job.

Hayek scathingly deconstructed this point in *The road to serfdom*, writing that:

> Socialism was to bring "economic freedom" without which political freedom was "not worth having." To make this argument sound plausible, the word "freedom" was subjected to a subtle change in meaning. The word had formerly meant freedom from coercion, from the arbitrary power of other men. Now it was made to mean freedom from necessity, release from the compulsion of the circumstances that inevitably limit the range of choice of all of us.

Exactly.

Recommended reading

Ecologist, The (1993) *Whose common future? Reclaiming the commons*, London: Earthscan.

Esteva, G. (2000) 'The revolution of the new commons,' in C. Cook and J.D. Lindau (eds) *Aboriginal rights and self-government: The Canadian and Mexican experience in North American perspective*, Montreal: McGill-Queen's University Press.

Esteva, G. (2010) 'Enclosing the enclosers,' in the Turbulence Collective (ed) *What would it mean to win?*, Oakland, CA: PM Press, pp 23-9.

Esteva, G. and Prakash, M. (1998) *Grassroots postmodernism*, London: Zed Books.

Fukuyama, F. (1992) *The end of history or the last man*, New York: Free Press.

Galeano, E.H. and Posada, J.G. (2000) *Upside down: A primer for the looking-glass world*, New York: Metropolitan Books.

Kingsnorth, P. (2003) *One no, many yeses: A journey to the heart of the global resistance movement*, London: Free Press.

Kohr, L. (1992) 'Size cycles,' *Fourth World Review*, vol 54, pp 10–11. (First published in *El Mundo*, San Juan de Puerto Rico, 1958.)

Mpofu, E. (ed) (2011) *Counseling people of African ancestry*, Cambridge: Cambridge University Press.

Polanyi, K. (1944) *The great transformation*, New York: Rinehart.

Marcos, S. (2001) *Our word is our weapon*, New York: Seven Stories Press.

Steger, H.A. (ed) (1984) *Alternatives in education*, Munich: Wilhelm Fink Verlag München.

SIX

The reclamation of the commons

Two billion people were labelled 'underdeveloped' overnight in the postwar era. With the launching of global development, they were placed in the undignified position of those who have started on a road that others know better, a way towards a goal that others have reached, a one-way street.

They were not underdeveloped. In Mexico, President Lázaro Cárdenas observed the effects of the crisis of 1929. He had a dream of a country of *ejidos* and small industrial communities, electrified, with sanitation, in which goods were produced for the purpose of satisfying the needs of the people, in which machinery was used to reduce people's toil. In India, Gandhi did not want merely to nationalize British domination; he was convinced that Western civilization was a curable disease. He wanted *Hind-swaraj*, India's home rule, a fully decentralized society enriching autonomously their old traditions with contemporary ideas and tools.

For 'underdeveloped' peoples, development connotes at least one thing: following the guidance of outside experts to escape from the vague, unspeakable, undignified condition that defines them. The development design appeared on the scene as the smarter, modern alternative to other political programs, such as those of Gandhi and Cárdenas, in which after centuries of colonization and domination people were expected to walk on their own feet, to follow their own roads. Through the notion of underdevelopment, they were offered the magical formula of the 'not-yet ... but will be.' Professor and later US National Security Adviser W. W. Rostow gave them a step-by-step, stage-by-stage formula in his 1960 *The stages of economic growth*, a 'non-Communist manifesto,' through which they could transform themselves from mere larvae into full-grown economic insects.

Since the 1980s, however, many peasants, urban marginal, and de-professionalized intellectuals have been trying to disconnect themselves from the dominant developmentalist institutions that permeate the global South. This profound social transformation is beginning to be called the revolution of the new commons. True, there is not a single word to fully express the diversity of social struggles attempting to create, at the grassroots, new ways of life and government. But calling them commons root these new shapes of society in an old tradition that express well their spirit and orientation.

Commons is a generic term for very different forms of social existence. The emerging new commons clearly differ from their predecessors. All these forms, both actualizations of ancient traditions and contemporary creations, are beyond the private threshold but cannot be defined as public spaces. They are not antique collective refuges or hunting preserves. They are not forms of property or land tenure. Specific ways of doing things, talking about them, and living them—art, *tecné*—express in themselves cultural traditions and recent innovations. Their precise limits (their contours, their perimeters) as well as their internal strings (and their straightjackets) are still insufficiently explored territory. They are gaining increasing importance in initiatives going beyond development. For more than 20 years political scientist Elinor Ostrom worked to call attention to them. Her 2009 Nobel Prize suggests that the intellectual establishment may finally be waking up to their importance.

An increasingly vigorous movement seeks to recover the enclosed commons and regenerate those who resisted its enclosure. These are not a small number of people: for example, 70 per cent of the world's fisheries still operate by way of the commons, and 85 per cent of the territory in Oaxaca, a state in southern Mexico, is in communal hands. There are also attempts to apply the rules of the commons—restricted and regulated access to common patrimony—to what are now considered global commons: water, air, forests, even seeds, all of them threatened by the savage exploitation of private corporations and their regimes of unfettered free access.

The term **commonism** refers to an increasingly extensive alliance between those who protect, reclaim, or create their own commons and those who want to protect what remains of the biosphere and remove themselves from individualistic consumerism.

In the tradition of the Iroquois nation, which brought together many diverse cultures throughout the northern US that were once in conflict, indigenous peoples in Australia, Latin America, Southeast Asia, the Arctic Circle, and throughout the world are cultivating the autonomy exercised in their communities. They give specific mandates to representatives who can come to agreement with others, much like them, through assemblies, real parliaments capable of giving form to social norms respecting them as common initiatives, and put them into practice. 'We are an assembly when we are together, we are a web when we are separated,' is how the National Indian Congress of Mexico expresses it. All the different indigenous communities and peoples live with autonomy, in their own settings, as a web, but they can come together and take decisions or shape accords in their assemblies.

Such commons–based models, never fully renounced in the global South, are now re-emerging in the global North. The Occupy movement, emerging right in the heart of global capitalism at the centers of New York and London, has operated as a commons. Before it was silenced by the 2001 terrorist attacks, the Seattle movement did too. Online social movements such as the open source software movement, the hacker movement, and even the new fountain of all knowledge, Wikipedia, operate on the commons principle. In terms of pure global reach and number of languages, Wikipedia is probably the most extensive commons the world has ever seen. But just as Quechuans sharing a small, isolated village high in the Andes, Wikipedians make decisions slowly, consensually, and democratically in every sense of the word—despite their protestations that they are not a

---

democracy. Perhaps they don't want to be stained by association with the political democracies of our age.

Relocalization

The internationalization of the world economy, now in its final phases, is increasingly reflected in the system of global mass media. The homogenization of ways of living of wide minorities (but minorities nonetheless), in both North and South, is increasingly evident. These phenomena have been used as empirical support for the illusion that all people on Earth are being 'globalized'—a prospect that some perceive as a threat, others as a promise. Whether threat or promise, 'realists' incessantly argue for the unavoidability of globalization, and this new emblem seems to be renovating the exhausted illusions of development.

Such 'realists,' however, remain blind to the fact that far from being globalized, the real lives of most people on Earth are fantastically marginalized from any 'global' way of life. The social majorities of the world will never have access to the consumption patterns of the globalists. The world's social majorities will never subsist on restaurant food, have access to well-equipped schools and well-staffed hospitals, check into a hotel room with an en suite bath, or drive SUVs as family cars. The globalists will have depleted the world's resources long before that could ever happen. Blaming the victims, through the euphemism of the 'demographic problem,' merely adds insult to injury.

Although some of the people marginalized from the amenities of modernity are still struggling to be part of the world's globalized minorities, many more have abandoned such illusions. In doing so, they are rediscovering their own culturally specific, alternative definitions of ways of living well, visions that are feasible in their own local spaces. Renouncing universal definitions of the good life as 'the American dream,' they are starting to protect themselves from the threats of modernity by rooting themselves more firmly in their soil, their local commons, in cultural spaces that belong to them and to which they belong. They are not ignoring the global phenomena that continually intrude on their lives, but delinking from them with ingenuity and effectiveness. They are escaping the globalization of their marginality by turning to *localization*, not localism or isolationism but a rediscovery of the authenticity of place. People firmly rooting themselves in their own place are today increasingly open to others like them, also localized, to create wide coalitions.

The time has come to recognize, as Leopold Kohr first revealed in his famous 1941 essay 'Disunion now: A plea for a society based upon small autonomous units,' that the true problem of modern age lies in the size, the scale acquired by many human creations. Instead of trying to counteract global forces through government or civic controls matching their overwhelming scale, he advised us "to reduce the size of the body politic which gives them their devastating scale, until they become once again a match for the limited talent available to the ordinary mortals of which even the most majestic governments are composed," as he put it in his 1958 essay 'Size cycles.' In other words, said Kohr, "instead of centralization or unification, let us have economic cantonisation. Let us replace the oceanic dimension of integrated big powers and common markets by a dike system of inter-connected but highly self-sufficient local markets and small states in which economic fluctuations can be controlled not because national or international leaders have Oxford or Yale degrees, but because the ripples of a pond, however animated, can never assume the scale of the huge swells passing through the united water masses of the open seas."

In this move toward localism some European thinkers are reconceptualising the EU from a union of nation-states into a Europe of regions. But why not the same for Africa? Developmentalists have always argued that African states are too small, too powerless to succeed. Why not an Africa of regions? A free Biafra sitting next to a free Delta State sitting next to a free Lagos. Why not a dis-union of South Africa, followed by integration into an umbrella African Union? Localization means that lives are lived locally: the schools, the hospitals, the roads, the recreational facilities, all serve local needs and local desires, not national (or international) directives.

Once we reorganize society in this decentralized way we will be able to deal with the problems of formal sovereignty, which will then be posed in a different way. Just as indigenous nations around the world demand sovereignty in land, language, and legislation—not in the formation of armed forces, the collection of taxes, or the maintenance of border posts—so too can other communities demand sovereignty over day-to-day life without the need to fight wars of secession against each other and the center. Localization is the best defence against the worst effects of globalization, and at the same time the best disseminator of its best effects. No autonomous local school board wants the worst for its children; no local water board wants dirty water; no local health authority wants to allow the development of antibiotic-resistant tuberculosis.

Surely, in a fully localized world some local units will make mistakes, even become dysfunctional. But when the citizens of one town see the citizens of neighboring towns prospering ahead of them, they become very impatient with their own 'boards of government' or their own decisions. They are in control. Localization means accountability. Those who believe that central authority is necessary because it is more administratively efficient need only look to the US, the ultimate purveyor of globalization. How did the US become a safe, well-schooled, healthy country in the first 200 years of its existence? It relied on local school boards, local water boards, local police departments, and local health departments to implement national standards that were set largely by confederations of local authorities—not handed down from the federal or even the state level. Now that 21st-century America is tearing these local institutions apart, ordinary Americans are suffering the consequences.

Coming back to your senses

Alejandro Santiago, a Zapotec, left Teococuilco, his community in Oaxaca, Mexico, when he was nine years old. He became a professional painter and came back to his community only during the fiestas, when everyone was there. One day he came back when there was no fiesta and he found the reality of his village: empty, abandoned. Most of the people had left to go to the US. He did the same, only to experience what they experienced. During that trip he conceived the idea of remembering all those absent, a total of 2,501 people. He came back to his village, established his workshop, and with the help of some of those still around, created 2,501 clay sculptures representing their faces and traits.

In 2010, 600 sculptures from Santiago's collection were exhibited in San Agustín Etla, in the central valley of Oaxaca. The venue was a disused textile factory transformed by the painter Francisco Toledo into a gallery and a workshop. The factory was once imposed on the people with the support of the army, which was also needed to close it when its owners decided it was no longer economically desirable to run it.

Santiago's sculptures have been touring the world to wide acclaim. But the impact of development in Santiago's home village has been devastating. In a video projected with the exhibition, he asks himself: "Progress? Is it progress to cover the whole community with cement?" Nonetheless, Santiago himself has hope. The name of his exhibition is 'Alejandro Santiago and his talismans against development.'

The rumour

A rumor is roaming around in *barrios*, *pueblos*, neighborhoods, towns. Born in Lima, San Juan de Puerto Rico, Mexico City, and a thousand other places, it has now spread to France, Germany, Japan, and the US. The media do not know how to deal with it. It is expressed in gossip, jokes, half-words, winks, smiles, a rumour we cannot spell out. What if…?

Survival strategies? Mere subsistence? Sometimes invisible, sometimes seen as a 'problem,' for a long time the ugly face of modern society, useless hand-me-downs of nothing and nobody, sterile remnants of the past, the classical target of wars against poverty that have for so long been waged against them; suddenly, in the midst of the challenges of the electronic era, they got new visibility. Some have just discovered them as a 'solution.' Others find in them the last frontier of arrogance, the last territory to conquest. Still others insist that they are the last refuge of pure joy and candid freedom, but fear that it is only a refuge and that it will not last long.

But, what if...?

A new awareness

For those who are used to living on the margins of the world stage, the economic picture of the world was always both puzzling and ludicrous. To be qualified or disqualified as remnants of the past did not really bother them much, since they fully appreciated their traditions, their historical roots; 'people without history' like to reinvent history when needed, for their own purposes. To be identified for what they are not (not formal, not developed, not employed, not salaried, not legal, not taxpayers, not in national accounts, not a social class, not central, not organized) or for their lacks (of capital, of entrepreneurship, of political awareness and organization, of education, of infrastructure, of rationality), that is, not to be seen, was perhaps not very comfortable. But they thrived in that social invisibility, and broke it when they needed to.

What really shook them was being doomed to extinction. The perception that they must first be subordinated and then 'incorporated,' disappearing as distinct populations, was not at all an academic exercise.

In many cases, colonization severely damaged and disrupted their modes of life, but respected many of their traditions. Decolonization, ironically, was more of a threat. Suddenly the light of development shone bright on the underdeveloped, and dazzled them for a time. For the first few postwar decades they adopted an ambivalent reaction toward **incorporation**, that is, the prospect of becoming economic beings inserted into a world market. Trying to protect their environments and strengthen their modes of living, they sometimes resisted development. Other times, having been lured by the developers' promises, they clamoured for their full 'incorporation' into society. The incorporation succeeded—for some.

Then came the end of the development era, the 1980s crisis of development. If the 1970s were the years of confusion, with new labels for every economic day and new strategies for every political eve, the 1980s brought unmistakable clarity. What many always suspected but did not dare say became evident: development stinks. A new experts' establishment documented the facts they already knew. Their incorporation into the world market on purportedly equal and fair conditions was increasingly unfeasible, while the gap to be closed between the center and the margins was constantly widening. The 1980s, the lost decade for development, was also the decade of the forging of a new awareness about the myth of development, as the structural impossibility of achieving development goals was fully and publicly exposed.

It is difficult to realize today that in the 1970s serious experts, economists and politicians alike fully anticipated the impending catch-up of Latin America and the newly independent countries of Africa and Asia with the old centers of Europe and North America. Black power was ascendant in the US as in Africa— George Foreman and Muhammad Ali fought it out for the world heavyweight crown not in Madison Square Garden but in Kinshasa, Zaire. Oil nationalizations and the OPEC embargo had elevated tribes of Middle Eastern desert nomads into major international financiers. Brazil and Mexico grew by leaps and bounds. As the US invented and then exported 'stagflation,' the countries of the global South were booming.

When Paul Volker became chairman of the US Federal Reserve system in 1979 he promised "blood on the floor" in his battle to fight inflation—Latin American blood. Middle Eastern and African blood soon followed. The first five years of the 1980s threw the previous 30 years of social arrangements conceived to foster development into complete disarray. The middle classes of the global South, living proof of the feasibility of development, lost almost everything of what they considered to be their gains. Many people on the margins found themselves destitute of both their traditional environments and the crumbs they usually got from developers. Frustration, disillusionment, desolation, and rage spread everywhere.

In the midst of this turbulence, however, a new awareness of many people on the margins revived and reshaped their determination, allowing them to also reshape their resistance. They discovered new forms of opposing the processes creating scarcity—and scarcity itself. Their traditions of social solidarity, previously an obstacle for development, became a strength to be nurtured and cherished. Their renewed self-perception impelled them to value what they still had, in spite of development. They began to count their blessings. On reflection, they saw in the 1980s crisis of development both damage and turbulence, but also opportunities for regeneration.

In spite of development and its crisis, they somehow succeeded in protecting and enriching their autonomy. By making visible the ways in which they did this, the 1980s crisis enabled them to regain confidence in the modes of perception that they had previously been taught to disdain. The revelation of the bankruptcy of educational systems freed them to redefine their needs and desires for learning, no longer associating it with standard schools. The paralysis of transportation systems brought them back to their *barrios*, where they rediscovered their autonomy. What they need from the outside world they can access through their mobile phones. Brought back into their communities, they are talking again, expressing themselves through eyes, words, and touch, instead of trying to 'communicate' through officially sanctioned channels.

Where previously they had personalized their struggles against specific developers who promised the sky and failed to deliver, they came to see the world economy itself as a threat. In the new vision of a globalized economy, it became obvious that their very existence was a challenge to the world's great powers. When the paralysis of development gave them an opportunity for regeneration it became evident that they survived if and because, in spite of colonization and development, they had been able to keep the economy at their own margins. Now, the globalizers wanted to destroy entire nations for the sake of a coalmine or a palm oil plantation. But now the nations were ready for them.

After recognizing their ability to limit the world economy in their concrete spaces, it was possible for them to identify, among those fully subsumed into the economic logic, some concrete interactions also limiting the encroachment of the economy into their lives. 'Economization'—the creation of *Homo oeconomicus*—was not at all complete. To survive in their economic prison, the alleged economic beings of modern society needed to cling to realities other than the economic in which the economic logic of life must be incarnated for it to be able to exist. As a result, a concrete hope for new political coalitions loomed on the horizons of the marginalized.

Enclosing the enclosers

As a conceptual construction, economics strives to subordinate to its rule and to subsume to its logic every other form of social interaction in every society it invades. The world doesn't conform to the simplifications of economic models, and it is the world that must change, not the models. As a political design and project, economic history is a story of conquest and domination. Far from being an idyllic story of peaceful evolution towards ever-higher standards of living, the emergence of the economic society was a story of violence and destruction that in many parts of the world was downright genocidal. Resistance appeared everywhere, and was often successful—for a time.

As Ivan Illich claimed, the establishment of economic value requires the disvaluing of all other forms of social interaction and existence. Disvalue transmogrifies skills into lacks, commons into resources, people into labor, tradition into burden, wisdom into ignorance, autonomy into dependency. It transmogrifies autonomous activities embodying wants, skills, hopes, and interactions with others into needs whose satisfaction requires the mediation of the market. Helpless individuals, whose survival is necessarily dependent on the market, was not an invention of the economists, nor were they born with Adam and Eve, as the economists contend. They were historical creations. They were created by the economic project that required the redesign of humanity to fit the standardizing needs of the market. The transmogrification of autonomous people into disvalued economic individuals was in fact the precondition for the emergence of the economic society and must be constantly renewed, reconfirmed, and deepened for economic rule to continue. Disvalue is the secret of economic value. It cannot be created except with violence and against continuous resistance.

The economy's Faustian bargain is subject to two kinds of limits: structural impossibilities and political controls. In the 1970s some of the former were exposed, in fora such as the Club of Rome, and ecologists clamoured for the latter. We see where that has led. Even in the face of today's impending planetary ecosystem collapse, there are no effective political controls on the world economy. Instead, limits are being imposed by resistance rather than regulation. The world economy, which for 500 years has done nothing but expand, is being turned back on its exposed flanks by the action of thousands of small groups throughout the world. They are joined by a fifth column of people within the rich countries of Europe and North America of people who have organized to reject the domination of the economy over their lives. All these movements share one thing in common: a desire to subordinate the economy to human needs, rather than to adjust human needs to the demands of the economy.

For people on the margins of society this limitation of the economic sphere is not a mechanical reaction to the economic invasion of their lives. They are not Luddites. They see their resistance as a creative reconstitution of basic forms of social interaction in order to liberate them from their economic chains. They have thus created, in their neighbourhoods, villages, *barrios*, new commons allowing them to live on their own terms. In these new commons there are forms of social interaction that only appeared in the postwar era, but the people in them are the heirs of a diversified collection of commons, communities, and even whole cultures that have been destroyed by the coming of economic society. After the extinction of their subsistence regimes, they tried to adopt different patterns of accommodation to the new society. Forced into economic society by the seizure of their land or the prohibition of their ways of life, they are now **disembedding** from it.

For many of them, disembedding from the economic logic of the market has become a precondition for survival. They are forced to confine their economic interactions, which for some are very frequent and intense, to the public realm on the outside of their own modes of living. Remedying the damage done by development to their lives and environments imposes a heavy toil on people who live on the margins, but it also engenders creative opportunities and deep satisfaction. Dismantling economic forms of interaction inside their modes of living and keeping them on the outside frequently amounts to no more than giving up a threatening illusion. Escaping education, for example, is no more than the acknowledgment that education as such is only the economization of learning, which creates scarcity.

Peasants and grassroots groups in the cities of the global South are now sharing with people whose families long ago left the land the ten thousand tricks they have learned to limit the economy, to marginalize the economic creed or to refunctionalize and reformulate modern technology (especially mobile phones) to further traditional cultural ends. The crisis of development removed from formal economy payrolls many people who had already been educated in dependency on income and the market, people lacking a social setting that would enable them to survive without the market. The margins are now coping with the difficult task of relocating these people. This process poses great challenges and tensions to everyone, but also offers a creative opportunity for regeneration after they discover how mutually supportive they can be for each other.

This flanking manoeuvre of the marginalized threatens— promises—to enclose the enclosers. This double movement must be seen in perspective. On the one hand, the world economy has now incorporated roughly half the population of the world into modern market-dependent lives in which it is literally impossible to live and raise a family outside the market system. Seen from another perspective, after 500 years of relentless incorporation, often by force of arms, less than half of the population of the world has been fully incorporated into the market economy. According to International Labour Organization data, 60 per cent of the world's adults are employed, with roughly one third in the *informal* sector (although estimates vary widely). In other words, only about 40 per cent of the world's adults work in formal, paid employment—and many of them only part time.

Major developmentalist organizations such as the OECD, the IMF, and The World Bank, continue to promote the informalization of the labor market under the banner of **flexible labor markets**. When a clothing factory is dismantled in North Carolina, it isn't reassembled in Bangladesh. Instead, the production of clothing is outsourced to sweatshops that rely on webs of local homebound producers to complete many intermediate stages of production in small batches. On the one hand, this is a regression to some of the most extreme forms of labor exploitation of the Industrial Revolution. On the other hand, it is making global supply chains vulnerable to local action and social control. The enclosers of the commons are still nowhere near being enclosed themselves, but they are vulnerable, and under attack on all sides.

The 18th-century enclosure of the commons

Enclosure (or inclosure) refers to the dissolution of common lands accompanied by the abolition of common rights, including activities such as growing hay, grazing animals, cutting timber, or other forms of cultivation on communal land. Land enclosure describes the consolidation of previously common fields, wasteland, open country, and scattered strips into blocks and their allocation to new, registered owners.

In the UK the process of enclosure dates back until the medieval period; however, it accelerated dramatically in the 18th century as a series of parliamentary Enclosure Acts were passed. Today, we refer to the years 1750-1850 as the era of parliamentary enclosure in which more than 4,000 Enclosure Acts were passed by Parliament and about the same amount of land was consolidated without application to Parliament (through private acts of enclosure). In the final period (late 19th century) the enclosure movement had essentially succeeded in abolishing the previously dominant communal mode of agriculture.

Prior to enclosure, most arable land was organized into an open field system where peasants grew crops and grazed livestock on scattered individual plots. Although larger landholders held the bulk of the land, they did not legally own it and had to respect communal grazing and cultivation rights. Common rights included livestock grazing, foraging for pigs, gleaning, cutting hay, berrying, fuel gathering, and the use of other communal resources such as fish, timber, turf, and peat. Before enclosure, common land and common rights were key components of agriculture, not only in Britain, but also in many parts of Europe. The collective use of the commons and fallow grazing were usually controlled and regulated by village authorities or the lord's court.

Whereas the first wave of enclosure (15th-17th century) was driven by prospects for higher profits through a shift from cultivation to more lucrative sheep pasture, the second wave of enclosure was caused by the notion of 'agricultural improvement.' In the 18th century, privatizing land was seen as a way of making agricultural production more efficient and more profitable (especially from the perspective of affluent landowners). Enclosed land would allow landlords to charge tenants higher rents, produce greater amounts of food to feed a growing population, and generate larger profits.

Albeit the social and economic effects of land enclosure are highly controversial, it was without doubt a significant social and historical phenomenon. Neo-Marxist historians argue that land enclosure was encouraged by the wealthy landowning class and carried out largely at the expense of the poor. The compensation for small landholders was often not enough to offset the costs of fencing or hedging, and forced many to sell their newly acquired land. While enriching the wealthy, small tenant farmers had to migrate elsewhere, work on privatized crops for rich landlords or move to urbanized areas where they became dependent laborers in the Industrial Revolution.

The new commons

One of the most interesting facets of the ongoing regeneration in the new commons created by ordinary people outside the realm of the market economy is the recovery of their own definitions of needs. By strengthening forms of interaction embedded in the social fabric and breaking the economic principle of the exchange of equivalents, they are recovering their autonomous ways of living. By reinstalling or regenerating forms of trade operating outside the rules of the market, they are both enriching their daily lives and limiting the impact and scope of the commercial operations they still have to maintain. In doing so, they are also reducing the commoditization of their time and of the fruits of their effort.

Millions of new settlers have become rooted in their new commons all over the world's cities. Viewed as slums from the outside, they are teeming with life within. Modernization attempted to modernize these places under the banner of 'slum clearance,' but even where slums were cleared, modern housing was rarely built. Slum clearance entailed destruction, but not development. The promised cars, factories, shopping centers, and motorways were never built, the poor never 'housed.' As a result, most of the homes existing in megacities of the global South today have been built by the dwellers themselves. This experience implied the factual elimination, in the spaces for such dwellings, of the markets for Polanyi's 'fictitious' commodities: land, labor, and money.

The virtual elimination of the markets for land, labor, and money always imposed great tension and effort on slum-dwellers as on the whole of society. The new commons softened those tensions, limiting the intervention of the economy and public institutions into the dwelling activities of ordinary people to a more or less satisfactory level. A great variety of arrangements were put in operation, many of them within a configuration that fits very well the patterns of rural or urban dwellers to establish or regenerate their new commons.

At the depth of the 1980s crisis of development, in Mexico, the worst affected country, an earthquake struck. The 19 September 1985 earthquake killed as many as 40,000 people and left more than half a million homeless. Some 100,000 dwellings had to be built in a short time and in very restricted spaces in downtown Mexico City. Developers jumped on the opportunity to redefine housing policy in Mexico. With the help of national and foreign professionals and institutions, they pressed for a typical industrial-scale, master-planned solution. The people, however, thought otherwise. Without waiting for the state to meet their needs, thousands of earthquake victims began to build for themselves the two- and three-storey dwellings that were appropriate for the kinds of conviviality they wanted in their neighbourhoods. The center of Mexico City today bears physical witness to the contrast between this creative expression and the failure of the 'developments' imposed on many victims of the earthquake.

The experience, although limited in time, space, and results, illustrates the new political form of social movements coming from the margins. In spite of the dominant marketization of the economy, ordinary people on the margins of society have been able to keep alive another logic, another set of rules. In contrast with the market, the logic of the commons is embedded in the social fabric. The time has come to confine the economy to its place on the margins. We should all take inspiration from the rebuilders of Mexico City, the rebuilders of Chittagong in Bangladesh, the rebuilders of Banda Aceh in Indonesia, the rebuilders of Port-au-Prince in Haiti, and even the rebuilders of Fukushima in Japan, who, despite living in one of the world's most developed and infrastructure-rich countries, have taken it into their own hands to rebuild their homes and businesses in the face of government paralysis. The new commons, born of need under conditions of extreme stress, are now expanding in response to people's equally important needs for belonging.

—

New social movements for a new era

The rumour of a new commons that is spreading in the *barrios*
and *pueblos*, the neighbourhoods and towns, the slums and
shantytowns, insinuated in the conversation of ordinary people
all over the world, is based on the experience of people's long
struggle to safeguard their localized freedom and autonomy.
They recognize that there are permanent tensions and conflicts
between their autonomous forms of existence and the prevailing
order in the national states, surrendered to the world economy
in all its political guises: liberal democracy, corporative state
or personal, theocratic or class dictatorship. They dream of
modalities of social organization more favourable to the lives they
are already living, today. They need a new legal order, based on
full respect and recognition of their new commons. They also
need a new social frame, to implement the transition from social
consensus—proper for homogenized individuals, for economic
beings—to social agreement—proper for differentiated groups,
for associated people in their new commons.

The structural impossibilities of development are not absolute
deterrents: here and there development is still feasible, and
everywhere development efforts are still under way, since
developers are weakened but not dead. The middle classes of
the global South still clamour to recover both their standards
of living and their expectations, and some are doing both. All
over the world, economy still occupies the center of the political
stage, whose fundamental challenge is still defined, by scholars or
politicians, as the discovery of the appropriate combination of
plan and market. Economists sit in government; anthropologists,
linguists, sociologists, artists, writers, historians, and other students
of the 95 per cent of the human experience that is not subsumed
within the economic sphere far outside it.

Competitiveness, modernization, the information revolution,
and 'green' development are still the slogans of the day, formulated
as a promise to spread prosperity to the last corner of the
planet. These slogans are tightly tied to recommendations for
strengthening the planned economy or the market economy, for

reinforcing the privileged role of the economy in politics, for fully subordinating society to the rules of the economic law of scarcity. These slogans are already flooding the mass media, which is still the central stage of politics, and that identifies which actors, candidates, governments, or political parties can be considered legitimate by the passive consumer population. Voters, denied any real representation, are increasingly discouraged but see little alternative but to continue to entrust the administration of the economy to the economists and their paymasters, the bankers.

All this poses a great threat to ordinary people. The internal strength of their new commons seems fragile when confronted with the disruptive impact of the economic forces still in operation. Some people, tired of their Sisyphean effort, are surrendering to the economy and thus weakening the still tenuous new commons they had helped organize. The universality of formal suffrage is irrelevant, if not harmful, to the flourishing of the commons when the representativeness of executive, legislative, and judiciary authority is concentrated on the selection of administrators for counterproductive economic institutions that operate under the dictatorship of professionals. The people may select the driver, but they do not select the machine or its path. Having selected the driver, however, people feel some obligation to obey the machine, even if the machine is locked on a collision course with their homes and their livelihoods.

As electoral democracy is increasingly perfected in formal procedures to ensure the universality and effectiveness of suffrage, it becomes increasingly weaker in content. To succeed in the creation and maintenance of their commons, ordinary people thus need to modify the fundamental political issues of society, reshaping every aspect of democracy in order to create a substitute for the democratic despotism now reigning everywhere. Electoral democracy, while in most ways preferable to military dictatorship, has showed itself in most cases to be no more responsive to the needs or the will of the people. 'Our dreams don't fit into your ballot box,' was the 2012 rallying cry of the *indignados* in Spain.

———

The new dynamics of the commons, according to the rumour roaming around the *barrios* and *pueblos*, does not appear as a utopian design or a universal political proposal that should be carried forward or become generalized. It stems from many concrete experiences that have made dreams material and rekindled hopes among those who live on the margins of economic societies and constitute their majorities. Formal, representative democracy works as a political umbrella for the new commons only if and when the mandate of the legitimately chosen representatives is limited and concentrated on supporting the new commons. This reformulation of the state and of social institutions, turning upside down the domination of the economy over society and instead confining economics to the margins, is only possible with the involvement of extensive citizens' coalitions. The order of genesis must be society—politics—economy, not as it is today economy—politics—society.

In the *barrios* and *pueblos* of the world, in Africa and Asia as in Latin America, spaces of freedom have been spawning where autonomy and the art of living are being exercised more fully. The Arab Spring is nothing if not a people's movement, and seems to be only at the beginning of the profound transformation defining it. It would be very interesting for those who are still immersed in the center of economic societies, immersed in the dependence on the market, to be able to witness their experiences and listen to their arguments. The market-bound would soon find out that they are not being invited to a return to some new stone age: any slum quarter of Nairobi or Jakarta is more culturally vibrant than all but the most sophisticated towns and suburbs of middle America. How can a person whose main center of community is a privately owned shopping mall—or worse, the local supermarket car park—look down on the poverty of anyone anywhere in the world? They are being called on to commence a constant and free enrichment of their lives.

What ordinary people, the marginalized but majority people of the world today, do in their communal spaces cannot be defined as merely a survival strategy, even if for them being protected from the economy is often a matter of life or death. Neither is their rejection of the market a backwards-looking attachment to a way of life devoted to 'mere' subsistence, an expression that synthesizes prejudices about such ways of life by connoting living conditions exposed to severe privations. Even those who accept that the initiatives of people on the margins may be more adequate for the sustenance of life than the efforts associated with development often refuse to see a living ideal in what marginalized peoples are doing. They would rather believe that some magic formula of development will allow, some day, the achievement of better conditions for all—if only we can hit on the right formula. Still others maintain an attitude of realistic scepticism and a certain degree of cynicism, recognizing the limited capacities of economic societies to secure welfare and justice for all, but accepting the fact as the way things are in real life.

Before the crisis of development and the resurgence of the commons, traditional peoples all over the world were strongly attracted to modernity. Existing in the world, they shared in the 20th-century love affair with technology. The experience of development, however, illuminated the dark side of modernity more starkly to them than it did to most others. In their newly reemerging commons, they have not translated this experience into Luddite fundamentalism or into folkloric conservatism. They have perceived the need to prudently take advantage of technological change. Many uneducated but highly learned peasants know, for example, that the old technology of slash and burn is now entirely inappropriate for the limited spaces they now have to sow. Today it is the developers who slash and burn, clearing pristine rain forest for grazing land or palm oil plantations, not the recently labelled 'primitive' indigenous peoples.

Modern-day peasants also know that industrial fertilizers and agrochemicals may be very harmful to their health and to the soil. Not for them the tortured soils of the American Midwest. They are now combining their ancient knowledge of microclimates with the more recent innovations of agronomy to develop sustainable methods. The practice of recycling industrial

—

products and of bootlegging have given valuable lessons to those who undertake these activities in the grassroots *barrios* within the cities, not only because of the opportunity they have had to master the technological secrets of industrial gadgets, but also because at the same time they have been able to keep their distance from them, de-mystifying the magic of wrappings and brands. Ordinary people living on the margins of the world economy are increasingly incorporating a careful selection of the industrial technologies that are useful to them, often after reformulating their use or design, as well as creating a constant flow of new technical or technological innovations.

The new commons are not forms of bare survival or devices for ensuring mere subsistence. They are contemporary ways of life, sound spaces for comfortable living, sociological novelties that activate traditions and reappraise modernity. They have been conceived in an era in which all that people need to be able to delight in living can easily be provided for within the technical means now available. They have also been conceived for an era in which non-economic ways of providing for human needs will allow people to look freely for what they want with dignity and wisdom. They have been created to leave behind an era in which the explicit goal of unlimited improvement was the smokescreen for the concentration of privilege and the license to impose every kind of suffering on the social majority for the sake of its own good.

The new commons, created by ordinary people, herald the dawn of a new era whose nature is the end of privilege and license. The time has come to listen to these people, to celebrate with them the adventure they have already started. The new commons can be better than the old commons, and serve a higher purpose. The old commons ensured every individual the means of physical subsistence. The new commons offer every society the opportunity for true fulfilment, for a convivial society in which friendship and graceful playfulness in human interaction may flourish. No developer can seriously offer anything near this condition. But the new commons is not some kind of utopian promised land. It is not a utopia because it already has a place in the world. It is happening. And it is happening now.

Recommended reading

Birchfield, V. (1999) 'Contesting the hegemony of market ideology: Gramsci's "good sense" and Polanyi's "double movement,"' *Review of International Political Economy*, vol 6, no 1, pp 27-54.

Ecologist, The (1993) *Whose common future: Reclaiming the commons*, London: Earthscan.

Gorz, A. (1997) *Farewell to the working class: An essay on post-industrial socialism*, London: Pluto Press.

Illich, I. (1977) *Toward a history of needs*, New York: Pantheon.

Illich, I. (1980) 'The new frontier for arrogance,' *Development*, vol 22, no 2/3, pp 96-101.

Illich, I. (1982) *Gender*, New York: Pantheon.

Kohr, L. (1957) *The breakdown of nations*, London: Routledge.

Kohr, L. (1992) 'Size cycles,' *Fourth World Review*, vol 54, pp 10-11.

McKnight, J. (1985) *The careless society: Community and its counterfeits*, New York: Basic Books.

Nandy, A. (1983) *The intimate enemy: Loss and recovery of self under colonialism*, Delhi: Oxford University Press.

Ostrom, E. (1990) *Governing the commons: The evolution of institutions for collective action*, Cambridge: Cambridge University Press.

Polanyi, K. (1944) *The great transformation*, New York: Rinehart.

Sahlins, M. (1972) *Stone age economics*, New York: Aldine de Gruyter.

Verhelst, T.G. (1987) *No life without roots: Culture and development*, London: Zed Books.

SEVEN

Epilogue: a role for development scholars and practitioners

After arguing throughout this book against the entire development enterprise, we should explore the extent to which development scholars and practitioners may or may not have a productive role to play in making the world (and its worlds) a better place. We assume that most of them are idealists motivated by compassion and the desire to do good, but are they doomed to either cynicism or hypocrisy? We hope not. What should they do? Should they become 'experts' (those with the ability to transform any situation into a 'problem' whose 'solution' always includes their expertise)? Or should they abandon their professions in despair, if they become convinced of the awful picture of the actual practice of development presented in this book?

The world is not lacking in problems. The conundrum is that most of the problems cannot be solved within the developmentalist framework, but outside it. Sure enough, the newly minted development expert will find no shortage of potential 'clients' in the poor and middle-income countries of the global South, not only international institutions, governments, or corporations in need of their services but also people who want 'development' no matter what is sold under that guise, people who are eager to accept the gifts offered to them, including, of course, technical help. We have no doubt, however, that they will confront sooner rather than later the kinds of resistance described here. In our own conversations with development veterans we have heard repeatedly of the 'ungrateful' and 'ignorant' people who seem neither to appreciate nor to understand the benefits being offered to them by benevolent charities, agencies, and an endless array of NGOs.

We find this troubling because we are convinced that the impulse that brought them to the theory or practice of development was in most cases a deep, serious commitment with ideas of justice and social change. Our hope is that these impulses may lead future generations of development students, scholars, and practitioners in another direction, if they are ready to learn the lessons of the last 60 years and, more importantly, if they are ready to listen to the people themselves.

A story

In 1992, on the commemoration of 500 years of the 'discovery' of the American continent, the monarchs of Spain came to see it for the first time. On visiting Oaxaca, in the south of Mexico, they were received in a very formal ceremony by Marcos Sandoval, a Triqui, in the name of the 16 indigenous peoples of Oaxaca who had been subjugated by the Spaniards 500 years before. Full of respect and hospitality, Sandoval welcomed them to this 'other' old world. He said (in Spanish, translated here to English):

> 'We use this occasion to tell the Western world that our way of life has been essentially communitarian, with solidarity, with a profound respect for the land, our mother, which protects and nourishes us; that is why our heart suffers when we see how it is damaged, destroyed by greed and ambition, when it is denied to their ancestral owners, when its natural equilibrium is broken with so many industrial products.

> 'We have been studied with the Western perception, in its different forms, but we have not been understood; the West imposes on us its form of development, its civilization, its way of seeing the world and relating to nature, thus denying

all the knowledge generated by our different peoples. We have domesticated the corn, that sacred plant which gave us existence, and we continue improving it. But even so, whenever an agronomist comes to our towns, he tells us that the corn numbered and produced in his research center is better; if we build a house with our knowledge and materials, an architect comes to tell us that a dignified house can only be built with industrial products; if we invoke our old gods, someone comes to tell us that our faith is superstitious.'

¡Basta! said the Zapatistas in 1994. Enough! Are we ready to listen?

Between justice and survival

Justice demands that the peoples of the Southern countries of the world should enjoy the freedom to consume at the levels enjoyed (if that is the word) by the peoples of the North. Survival demands that the peoples of the Northern countries of the world should be limited to consuming at the levels endured (if that is the word) by the peoples of the South. Politically conscious and morally responsible people have, for many years, been tortured by this dilemma.

They cannot find a way out. They prepare estimates with increasing perplexity. They recognize without reservation the responsibility of the Northern countries for the present and looming destruction of nature and culture. They know that their socially irrational consumption is the main source of the world's ecological predicaments. But they offer no solutions. No feasible sacrifice in the living arrangements of the North could bring them to a level that would make use of the world's agricultural land, fisheries, freshwater supplies, mineral resources, atmosphere, or ecology in a sustainable way. And so long as they are used in an unsustainable way, it is the South that must sacrifice to meet the appetites of the North.

You are damned if you do and damned if you don't. This popular saying expresses the dilemma currently confronted by the majority of the inhabitants of the planet: neither one way nor the other will they be able to live in the living conditions offered as a model for many years. Truman's promise to the 'underdeveloped areas,' the promise of "more food, more clothing, more materials for housing, and more mechanical power," literally, the promise of "more ... more ... more," is not just unfulfilled; it is unfulfillable.

In addition to perplexity, this fact generates rage, anger, frustration, and a feeling of impotence. Many people in the South believe that the 'good things in life' are being withheld, that they are there for the giving but are not being given. However, for an increasing number of people in the South this dilemma is seen as irrelevant. The global monoculture of development is still being imposed, day after day, throughout the whole world. This is undeniable. But it is also undeniable that many people are instead affirming or reaffirming their own ways of living well, day after day, throughout the whole world. They may be ignored, but they will not be denied.

Even many of those who previously gave up any hope of safeguarding their pre-development ways of life are now struggling again. Claiming respect for the autonomy of their new commons, many people are attempting, first of all, to regenerate their notion of living well, and second, to perceive it, once again, as a cultural expression, alive and changing, of a community well rooted in its tradition and soil. This position should not be confused with the contemporary search, now fashionable, for 'alternative lifestyles.' It is rather a new search for freedom, justice, localization, and radical pluralism. It is based on the assumption of cultural relatedness, which is opposed to both exclusive universalism and muddy cultural relativism. It claims, for the peoples constituting the majority of the Earth's population, what they have been denied for the last 500 years: autonomous routes to their unique, locally rooted lifestyles.

It claims the rights to human flourishing and to cultural endurance.

The peoples in the South will never be like the peoples in the North. They will never be able to 'develop,' on the terms laid out by Truman and all the other versions of the development enterprise, no matter how many of their cities, roads, governments, and consumers come to look like their Northern counterparts. Shanghai can only outbuild New York through a process by which China creates its own internal zones of severe exploitation that most outsiders never visit. For all of China to live like Shanghai would require a second world to provide the billions of low-wage workers who would be needed to service it.

The consciousness of these facts does not have to drive us to the cynical acceptance of injustice or the desperate, useless search for alternative means. It is a clear motive for celebration, if it is accompanied by a complete recognition of the 'other:' that is, if it is accompanied by the abandonment of the project for the Westernization of the world. Ideally, it should be accompanied by the abandonment of the project for the Westernization of the West itself. Instead of radically denying the 'other,' as has been done under the flags of civilization, colonialism, evangelization, industrialization, modernization, democratization, and development, the world must open to a new, radical pluralism. The one approach to life that is enshrined in the development dogma is at the same time unjust, inhospitable, and unsustainable. The many other approaches to life that oppose it may not all be just and sustainable, but at least they are not unjust and unsustainable by construction.

How can I help?

"The times in which helping still helped, certainly in the form of 'development assistance'... are irrevocably past," wrote Marianne Gronemeyer for *The development dictionary*. "These days," she added, "help can usually only be accepted if accompanied with threats; and whoever is threatened with it had better be on their guard." And she immediately quotes Henry David Thoreau:

> If I knew for a certainty that a man was coming to my
> house with the conscious design of doing me good, I
> should run for my life ... for fear I should get some of his
> good done to me.

In her essay, Gronemeyer compiled the lessons expressed in
Thoreau's paradox: help as a threat. This perception is, of
course, contrary to common sense, but today the experience of
millions of people has been well documented: all kinds of stories
demonstrate how food aid can lead to hunger and health aid
can lead to sickness. It need not be, it shouldn't be and yet it is.
Helping is a big business. Hunger and epidemics are powerful
alibis for subsidies in the North, which repeated crises have
not been able to dismantle, despite their increasingly evident
counterproductivity.

We do not argue that hungry people should be left to starve,
or that sick people should be left to die. Sometimes acute relief
is necessary, and sometimes the US Navy is the only organization
in the world with the technical capacity to provide that relief.
But such situations are rare. When an earthquake strikes, by all
means, airlift heavy earthmoving equipment and emergency tents
to the crisis zone. And then, one month later, leave.

Over 300,000 people died in the 12 January 2010 Port-au-
Prince earthquake in Haiti. Over the next two weeks rescue
workers—all rescue workers, Haitian and foreign—saved 130
people from the rubble. The cholera introduced by the rescue
workers, however, killed more than 3,000. While we may
legitimately rejoice in the rescue of the 130, on balance, was
the international intervention a success? The helpfulness of the
international intervention is, at best ... not obvious.

Two days after the earthquake, US President Barack Obama
declared that:

> 'I have ordered a swift, coordinated, and aggressive effort
> to save lives in Haiti. We have launched one of the largest
> relief efforts in recent history. I have instructed the leaders
> of all agencies to make our response a top priority across

the federal government. We are mobilizing every element of our national capacity: the resources of development agencies, the strength of our armed forces, and most important, the compassion of the American people. And we are working closely with the Haitian government, the United Nations, and the many international partners who are also aiding in this extraordinary effort.'

In light of the (by all accounts) uncertain palliative impact of a full-scale intervention by the most powerful country in the world operating a mere 1,000km off its coast in a country that is (for all practical purposes) a colonial protectorate, it is hard to imagine that other international interventions do much good. Some, perhaps. We do not judge; we merely observe.

If you are an idealistic European with a passion for Africa, such a passion that you want to dedicate your career (and perhaps your life) to the betterment of the lives of Africans, by all means pursue a degree in development studies and go to work in development. Become an activist, start an NGO. Focus your life's work on reducing meat consumption in Europe so as to put less strain on world food prices; promote food localism so that fewer Africans are dispossessed to make way for commercial farms; lobby against environmentally destructive biofuels subsidies; change European living patterns from car-dependent suburbs to car-free cities; pass laws to keep European toxic and nuclear wastes in Europe instead of being exported; prevent the release of genetically modified organisms into the environment; prohibit European factory boats from harvesting in African waters; eliminate the intellectual property provisions in trade treaties that prevent African producers from manufacturing patented drugs, etc., etc., etc. Then indulge your passion for Africa by travelling in Africa as a tourist, carefree, fully enjoying your time on the continent.

The bedrock principle that all prospective helpers of all kinds should always follow is very simple: 'first, do no harm.' The preventative European interventions above are very unlikely to cause serious harm in Africa and will certainly do much good for the world as a whole. Development work in the field, however, is rife with unintended consequences—as the introduction of cholera to Haiti in 2010 demonstrated.

If you must work in the field, work to support self-determination and the autonomous projects of self-organizing communities. Many people in the global South are unfamiliar with the institutions of the global North that they must either deal with or resist. They may not have easy access to the tools and techniques they need to navigate a social environment that, like it or not, is often dominated by foreign governments, foreign militaries, and huge multinational corporations. People are rooting themselves more than ever in their physical and cultural spaces, but instead of isolating themselves, entrenched in old customs and traditions, they are opening hearts, minds, and arms to create wide coalitions with others like them in the open world. A committed outsider may operate as a hinge or at least a link in the formation of such coalitions.

Direct help, on the other hand, is less likely to yield unambiguous results. The Australian surgeon who sets bones in East Timor can see every day the impact of her good work; she may not see their unintended consequences, which in her case may be small. But when Jeffrey Sachs and his colleagues at the UN spend US$100 million to create model Millennium Villages across a dozen African countries, the unintended consequences are likely to be ... large. In the development industry, however, even the UNDP (annual revenue: US$4 billion) is small potatoes compared to Royal Dutch Shell (annual revenue: US$470 billion). When Shell 'develops' Nigeria by drilling offshore for oil, the unintended consequences aren't even obscure: the rise of private armies, the forced displacement of indigenous communities, pollution everywhere. Now *that's* development.

Two stories and a conclusion

In the 1960s, Ivan Illich became known for his increasing opposition to the presence of any and all North American 'do-gooders' in Latin America. He actively tried to obtain the voluntary withdrawal of all North American volunteer armies from Latin America: missionaries, Peace Corps members, students in service learning programs, and others. Invited as the keynote speaker to the annual convention of the Conference on Inter-American Student Projects, in Cuernavaca, Mexico, on 20 April 1968, he pronounced a now famous speech ('To hell with good intentions') that constitutes a radical indictment of any voluntary service activity, and in particular, any international service 'mission.' He told his audience:

> 'I am here to challenge you to recognize your inability, your powerlessness and your incapacity to do the "good" which you intended to do. I am here to entreat you to use your money, your status, and your education to travel in Latin America. Come to look, come to climb our mountains, to enjoy our flowers. Come to study. But do not come to help.'

Development students, scholars, and practitioners would do well to read, heed, and remember Illich's remarks, although this is easier said than done. We—we peoples of all places, North and South, scholars and laypeople alike—are so indoctrinated by the development ideology that it is almost impossible for us to step back and to see the world as it is, rather than as we have been educated to believe it is, or should be. We need constant reminding to look, listen, and learn rather than to ignore, instruct, and impose. Even so celebrated an academic and activist as Wolfgang Sachs admits that he needs reminding. The editor of *The development dictionary*, he wrote in his essay 'The archaeology of the development idea:'

> I wanted to kick myself, but then my observation seemed to be the most natural in the world. It was six months after the catastrophic earthquake of 1985, and I had spent the day walking through Tepito, a rundown neighborhood near the center of Mexico City, inhabited by common people but threatened by speculators. We expected ruins and resignation, depression and dirtiness, but our observations

proved different; there was a proud neighborhood spirit, vigorous activity, with small construction cooperatives all over. We saw a flowering underground economy.

But at the end of the day, a little lightheartedly, I finally said: "All of this is very good, but at the end of it all these people are terribly poor." Immediately one of our companions exclaimed emphatically: "We're not poor, we're Tepitans!" What a reprimand! Why did I make such an offensive remark? I had to admit to myself, with shame, that the clichés of the development philosophy had sparked this voluntary reaction.

Alfonso Hernández, the Tepitan, knew very well what he was saying. He immediately explained that he could also call Wolfgang poor if he applied the same comparison Wolfgang was making. Wolfgang lacked many of the things Alfonso had, as Alfonso lacked many of the things Wolfgang had. But he refused to reproduce the attitude. He added: "You are German. I am Tepitan. Let's respect each other."

We share today many predicaments. The facts described in this book affect everyone, perpetrator and activist alike. We all need to react. And now. If the readers of this book are as we assume them to be, people interested in working to make the world a better place, there is room for them, for their activity, for you, for your activity. Your first step should be to carefully study the real history of the place you want to go, and specifically the history of what your own country and your own society did and continue to do in that place. And then go and see for yourself.

Perhaps you will not end up doing what you imagined when you started your preparation for the adventure. But you can have a fulfilling and rewarding experience. You should go where your heart leads you, and then ask, and listen. Let the locals—whoever they are—discover your talents and skills and what you can do in their place. Explore with them how and why their struggle is also your struggle. Trust your imagination more than your technical knowledge in discovering how can you support and even participate in self-determination, self-government, and independent initiatives. Most of all, be ready to fully engage in a world beyond development, openly challenging your own hard-won expertise. And enjoy!

Glossary

basic needs
An approach to development that focuses on the formal eradication of absolute poverty by ensuring that people have access to water, food, clothing, and shelter.

biocapacity
A quantification of the biological resources that an ecosystem provides; the Earth's biocapacity measures the planet's ability to produce sufficient resources and to absorb enough waste to sustain human life.

biofuel
A type of fuel that is derived from renewable resources (for example, plant biomass, wheat, corn, sugar, vegetable oil, animal fat, waste).

charter cities
An attempt to establish privately planned cities with their own laws and tax systems, divorced from the larger societies in which they are embedded.

commonism
A word that adds to commons owned by people the group aspirations for social commons (such as public education), networked commons (such as open source software), and ecological commons (for example, fresh water).

Copenhagenize
A verb that loosely describes attempts to revitalize human habitats, especially in urbanized areas; it includes the reduction of traffic in city centers, the greening of rooftops, and the promotion of small-scale housing.

décroissance
A French word that translates as 'de-growth;' it is a political, social, and economic critique of growth that includes a pledge to decouple humanity's wellbeing from the imperative of infinite economic expansion.

development
A controversial term that has meant different things in different eras but is usually used today to represent an industrialized, consumerist, materialist, and capitalist vision of economic and social success.

development decades
Originally, a series of thematic decades declared by the United Nations to be dedicated to development, beginning with the 1960s; more loosely, a rhetorical tool for promoting new development programs.

developmentalist
An adjective describing ideologies of development that promote convergence to US economic and social models as the goal of development policy.

disability adjusted life year (DALY)
A single metric that combines two major measures of disease burden: mortality and morbidity; technically, DALYs are computed by adding up the years lived with disability (YLD) and the years of life lost (YLL).

disembedding
A reaction against forced integration into the market economy that is characterized by the withdrawal of people's labor and consumption into non-market spheres.

double movement
Karl Polanyi's omnibus term for the expansion of the laissez-faire market economy combined with the countermovements to protect people from the negative effects of a free market regime provoked by the expansion of the market.

ecological footprint
A methodology used to quantify the total amount of land and water required to sustain human population; ecological footprints are measured in global hectares (gha) and can be used to determine ecological deficit or surplus by measuring the Earth's biological capacity against human demand.

ecological growth criticism
An intellectual movement to draw attention to the ecological limits of the Earth's biological capacity through criticism of systems of growth that depend on the extraction of (non-renewable) natural resources and the absorption of tremendous amounts of waste.

ecological overshoot
This occurs when human demand exceeds the Earth's capacity to regenerate the resources required to sustain the human population.

enclave
A geographical entity that is surrounded by an economically and sometimes politically distinct entity; in many countries Westernized central business districts are enclaves surrounded by poverty.

exchange rates
Market or official rates at which members of the public can exchange one currency into another.

Federal Reserve
The US Federal Reserve System, the central bank of the US and the issuer of US dollars.

flexible labor markets
Labor markets with few protections for workers, making it easy for employers to employ them for part-time or irregular hours and to hire and fire them at will.

GDP (gross domestic product) per capita
A country's national income divided by its population; widely used as a rough indicator of development.

Gini index
The most widely used measure of inequality; a score of 0 indicates perfect equality while a score of 100 represents perfect inequality.

global hectare (gha)
A measurement unit that refers to the Earth's biocapacity; it represents the average productive and absorptive capacity of a hectare of biologically productive land or water.

Great Charter of the Forest
The Charter forced on King John at Runnymede in Britain in 1215 and 1225 that established popular rights over common land and thus ensured English commoners the means of economic survival.

green efficiency
The attempt to maximize output levels by simultaneously minimizing units of input and ecological deficits.

gross domestic product (GDP)
The sum total of goods and services produced or provided within a country's borders.

gross national product (GNP)
The sum total of goods and services produced or provided by the residents of a country; roughly equivalent to gross domestic product plus income earned abroad and minus income sent abroad.

harmonious society
The goal of China's 11th five-year plan (2006-10); the avowed aim was to reduce inequality and to ensure a reasonable standard of living for all.

incorporation
Integration, usually forced or coerced, into the global market economy of those who had previously lived largely outside it.

indigenous
An adjective describing the peoples and cultures existing in a place before the creation of today's nation-states.

informal sector
A sector of the economy, predominant in many poor countries, characterized by reliance on common resources, family ownership of resources, small scale of operation, labor-intensive and adapted technology, skills acquired outside the formal school system, and unregulated and competitive markets.

International Monetary Fund (IMF)
A Washington-based financial institution founded in the wake of the Bretton Woods conference in 1944; the IMF's official goal is to promote international cooperation among its 188 member states relating to the stabilization of exchange rates, expansion of free trade and provision of loans.

—

juridical pluralism
The doctrine that a plurality of legal cultures and legal systems can coexist in the same geographical and political space.

less-developed countries (LDC)
A term used to describe poor countries, incorporating the normative implication that their future 'development' is desirable.

life expectancy
The estimated average number of additional years an individual is expected to live based on existing sex and age-specific death rates in the individual's country of residence; typically, but not necessarily, evaluated at birth.

life table
A table of sex and age-specific death and survival rates for a given country in a given year.

localization
An alternative to both globalization and localism; it is an expression of the extended localist movement in which the people try to root more than ever in their own places while remaining open to others who are doing the same; a program of globally interconnected local identities.

majority world
A term used to describe the approximately 80 per cent of the world's population that lives outside North America, Western Europe, Japan, Australia, and New Zealand; closely associated with the *New Internationalist* magazine.

Malthusian
An adjective describing the belief derived from Thomas Malthus (1766-1834) that the population would always grow more rapidly than the available food supply, resulting in inevitable widespread starvation.

median
The value that is located in the middle in an ordered list of observations; median income is the income of the person at the middle of an income distribution.

Millennium Development Goals (MDGs)
A set of eight development goals that all United Nations members have agreed in principle to achieve by 2015, relating to poverty, education, gender, child mortality, maternal health, diseases, sustainability, and global partnership.

neoliberalism
A political philosophy, a set of economic policies, and a development theorem that has been re-promoting ideologies of classic 19th-century liberalism in contemporary settings; neoliberal policies include free trade, privatization, deregulation, and the expansion of the market sphere.

New International Economic Order
An unsuccessful attempt by poor and middle-income countries in the 1970s to shift the governance of the global economy toward macroeconomic stability and improved terms of trade for poor-country exports.

North American Free Trade Agreement (NAFTA)
A 1992 agreement (effective from 1994) to create a free trade and investment area covering Canada, Mexico, and the US.

North Atlantic Treaty Organization (NATO)
The system of US allies in North America and Europe.

official development assistance (ODA)
An OECD (Organisation for Economic Co-operation and Development) term that formally measures foreign aid provided to low- and middle-income countries by governments and intergovernmental organizations.

———

people's sovereignty
The tradition locating the idea of sovereignty within the people themselves, increasingly applied to ideas and practices in which the people take their lives into their own hands and adopt different forms of self-government.

postdevelopment
An intellectual movement deconstructing the normative association of development with improvement; Wolfgang Sach's 1992 *The development dictionary* is a key text (published by Zed Books).

precariat
A neologism mixing precarity and proletariat, increasingly used in Europe to allude to the situation of people who are losing the labor conditions they previously took for granted.

purchasing power parity (PPP)
A method of converting economic statistics from national currencies into US dollars that takes into account cross-national differences in prices and the costs of living; construed as an alternative to the use of exchange rates for this purpose.

radical pluralism
A humble human attitude acknowledging that no one can represent the totality of human experience and the pluralism of truth; associated with Spanish intellectual and priest Raimón Panikkar.

redevelopment
A trend in the 1990s to develop again what was mal-developed or became obsolete, in order to give development a new lease of life.

remittances
Financial transfers from migrants or foreign workers to their home countries with the aim of supporting families and relatives.

Rio Declaration
Officially the Rio Declaration on Environment and Development, a statement of 27 principles for sustainable development that was agreed at the United Nations Earth Summit in Rio de Janeiro in 1992.

Roosevelt, Franklin Delano
The 32nd President of the US (1933-45), author of America's 'New Deal' social welfare programs and President for most of the Great Depression and the Second World War; died in office and was succeeded by Harry S. Truman.

social growth criticism
A viewpoint that stresses the adverse effects of economic growth on social wellbeing and challenges the notion that growth and social wellbeing are inevitably related.

sovereignty
The exercise of independent authority; in political discourse, sovereignty is the self-determination of institutions made possible by the exercise or transfer of state authority.

Stalin, Joseph
Leader of the Soviet Union from the early 1920s through 1953, author of the Soviet Union's system of five-year plans and leader of the Soviet Union throughout the Second World War; led the Cold War against the US.

standard of living
A description of the ability to meet the necessities of everyday life within a given sociocultural context.

structural adjustment policies
Neoliberal economic policies in developing countries imposed as loan conditions by the International Monetary Fund (IMF), World Bank and other governmental or intergovernmental organizations.

sustainable development
Forms of development that take into account the wellbeing of both present and future generations.

System of National Accounts (SNA)
The accounting system sanctioned and managed by the United Nations through which gross domestic product and gross national product are calculated.

third world
Historically, the non-aligned countries, as distinct from the first world (the US and its allies) and the second world (the Soviet Union and its allies); more generally, the poor countries of the world.

Truman, Harry S.
The 33rd President of the US (1945-53), succeeded to the presidency on the death of Franklin Delano Roosevelt; ordered the atomic bombing of Japan and coined the modern usage of the term 'underdevelopment.'

United Nations
An intergovernmental organization of 193 member states, founded in 1945 as a permanent embodiment of the anti-fascist alliance; its primary mission is to promote cooperation in international peace, human rights, international law, and social progress.

Via Campesina
A transnational peasants movement, originating in Europe and Latin America, but now global in scope, advocating food sovereignty and localization in agriculture.

Walmartization
The transformation of richly textured person-to-person artisanal economies into generic modern economies dominated

by monolithic corporations; named after Walmart, the US multinational retailer.

Washington Consensus
A term coined in 1990 by economist John Williamson to describe the standard economic prescriptions of the three major Washington development institutions: the US Treasury, the International Monetary Fund, and The World Bank; closely identified with neoliberalism.

World Bank, The (officially, International Bank for Reconstruction and Development)
A Washington-based financial institution founded in the wake of the Bretton Woods conference in 1944; The World Bank's official goal is to promote international cooperation among its 188 member states relating to poverty reduction.

World Development Indicators (WDIs)
A statistical database published by The World Bank that includes development-related data for 214 countries and territories for the periods from 1960 to today.

World Economic Forum (WEF)
An international leadership non-governmental organization that holds a high-profile conference of the world's most powerful and influential individuals every January in the ski resort of Davos, Switzerland.

Zapatista
A noun or adjective referring to the Mexican anti-systemic commons-based movement, the Ejército Zapatista de Liberación Nacional (Zapatista Army for National Liberation), which associated its identity with the prestigious name of Emiliano Zapata, the peasant hero of the Mexican Revolution of 1910.

—

Index

Note: Page numbers followed by *g* refer to terms in the glossary.